WHAT PEOPLE ARE SAYING ABOUT
HOW TO WIN THE HEALTH CARE GAME

"Educating our employees about changes in healthcare is easier because of this book. It provides a historical background, offers real life examples and clearly explains why it is so important to learn the new definition of great health insurance coverage. This is a must read for all age groups so that unexpected health care costs never become a financial burden. Jon Warner is an expert who cares about the long term financial and medical health of people."
Greg Kelly President Kelly Automotive Group

"I have great respect for Jon Warner resulting from our many years of business collaboration. As a health insurance expert and creative thinker, Jon understands risk and corresponding costs. In his comprehensive style, he details the current state of health care with creative insights on insurance plan options. I hope you enjoy this book and find it as informative as I have."
Pepper Krach, EVP, M.F. Irvine Companies

"It took time for our company to embrace the concepts promoted in this book. Once we transitioned, it is the simplicity of the coverage and the opportunity to compare the cost of health care services that has been most eye opening. The answer to high quality, affordable and balanced health insurance is so very well explained in this book, along with ways to build retirement health care savings.

David Weinstein President Sunburst Property Group

"Education about health insurance trends is a daily part of my profession. What Jon Warner offers in his book is refreshing and easy to follow. He truly has a gift for simplifying complex topics. The concepts he describes are a pathway for excellent protection to help us all look at insurance in a new light financially and philosophically. I especially appreciated his people stories as they are realistic and personal. This book is a must read for my entire team."

Vicki L. Doulé Senior Director Capital Blue Cross

"I have successfully introduced the concepts in this book to many employers. They reduce their cost while their employees maintain excellent health insurance coverage and spend less. This book clearly explains how to design quality insurance coverage that is affordable in our changing world."
Matt Hayes Senior Account Executive Sovereign Insurance Group

"HOW TO WIN THE HEALTH CARE GAME should be mandatory reading for everyone involved in designing health care plan options. Jon Warner describes with great clarity changes occurring with the passage of the Affordable Care Act and includes vivid illustrations of health plan decision making by individuals at different life and economic stages. With the help of Jon's wisdom, an organization I led introduced the ideas presented here and was able to control cost plus adopt wellness standards that accrued to the financial benefit of the corporation and most importantly to the overall well being of our employees and their families."
F. Mark Gumz Retired CEO Olympus of the Americas

HOW TO WIN THE HEALTH CARE GAME

JONATHAN PIERPONT WARNER, CEBS

INTRODUCTION

FOREWORD by Kirk A. Putt

Background for Winning the Health Care Game

People Stories for Winning the Health Care Game

Effectively Winning the Health Care Game

INTRODUCTION

More Americans are paying attention to the real cost of health insurance. Historically the majority of premiums have been paid by our employers with cost awareness focused on how much we spend out of our pockets once we receive health care services. It used to be that many chose the most costly plan offered as the common thinking was the more expensive the better. Also, payroll contribution amounts were nominal and affordable.

Times have been changing with never ending premium increases. As payroll deductions for generous plans have risen, alternative plans with more out of pocket cost responsibility are becoming the new standard. Even though thousands of dollars in out of pocket cost may result if injured or sick, many feel they have no choice but to accept this burden and hope for the best.

Caring Americans believe that good coverage for health care needs is an American right like clean water and safe streets. What is then required is that premiums include a charge for normal health care needs including limiting the out of pocket cost of a doctor's visit to 20% of the total expense. It is cash flow friendly and easy when pre-paying in premiums to allow nominal copays when visiting the doctor or buying a prescription. Unfortunately this is becoming an increasingly expensive and inefficient luxury. It also eliminates options to save for future health care needs.

Premiums fall 15% to 30% when normal care needs are shifted back to the individual. For this reason Americans are increasingly transitioning to plans with upfront deductibles and coinsurance. Of course concern exists about cost as an excuse for not seeking medical help. Fortunately there is good news in that contemporary plan designs cover preventive care services at 100%, and if set up properly, affordability in paying for normal care needs can be maintained.

These opportunities are at the core of *How to Win the Health Care Game.* It should be of no surprise that this book examines how and when to use Flexible Spending Accounts (FSAs), Health Reimbursement Arrangements (HRAs) and Health Savings Accounts (HSAs) as protection for affording the out of pocket cost of deductibles and coinsurance. Turn now to pages 111 & 112 to view the savings potential for health care needs.

The Patient Protection & Affordable Care Act (PPACA), also known as The Affordable Care Act and Obamacare is building awareness about the real cost of health insurance. Once it became law, a 10 year transition began that is affecting every American's insurance coverage and standard for quality and efficient health care delivery.

Health insurance premiums are now listed on the annual Form W-2 Summary of Earnings for millions of workers because of the law. With the introduction of public and private Healthcare Marketplace Exchanges, selecting a plan now starts with understanding the full premium cost and then subtracting monetary subsidies provided by employers or the government to pay a portion of the premium cost.

Because higher premiums include pre-payment for normal care needs, the new world of health insurance selection includes considering:

1. Total premium expense
2. Net personal premium cost
3. Options to minimize out of pocket risk

There are intended and unintended consequences of the law that result in praise and disdain for this legislation. The fact that ill Americans can no longer be denied access to insurance because of a pre-existing condition is a welcome change. Accomplishing this requires an increase in taxes for all Americans who are covered under employer sponsored health insurance plans. Promises have been made about bending the cost curve once the law is fully implemented. Concern exists this means delays in receiving desired care due to the rationing of health care services.

The Affordable Care Act is prompting insurers to assume much higher usage of coverage. Double digit percentage premium increases result which is adding to the expectation that by 2020 a majority of working Americans will choose health insurance plans with sizable upfront deductibles and coinsurance. Winners will be the best educated, transferring premium savings into pre-tax emergency funds so money is set aside to pay future out of pocket costs when expensive care is needed. See pages 111 & 112.

The first section of *How to Win the Health Care Game* offers a historical perspective on health insurance in America along with explaining contemporary approaches and ways to efficiently reduce premium costs plus eliminate risk through pre-tax short and long term savings approaches.

The second section of *How to Win the Health Care Game* includes examples of cost efficient, quality decision making by employers and individuals when choosing between health insurance plans at various stages of work and family life.

The third section of *How to Win the Health Care Game* builds on this efficiency foundation offering insights into America's vast, complex and excellent health care delivery system.

All of us are likely to take advantage of health care services during our lifetime and most have already benefitted from the system if born in a hospital. Miraculous and amazing cures are available when we fall ill or are injured. The number of curative services offered today is awe inspiring compared with one generation ago, and we should anticipate even more amazing advancements in the years to come.

Fortunately most of us have an inconsistent need for costly health care services each year. What follows is a roadmap for maintaining quality and affordable insurance protection that allows tax efficient savings to be used for normal care needs, and the times when we need more costly care.

With this approach, when costly health care use occurs, cash flow is not a burden as savings exist, eliminating out of pocket risk. Should expensive care not be needed the funds become an asset to use for retiree health care costs including normal retirement expenses and Long Term Care, or to pass along to the next generation.

FOREWORD

I received a call notifying me that a young man I know was in a near fatal motorcycle accident and had to be airlifted to a trauma center. My initial reaction was concern about the well-being of the individual and his family. I was relieved to later receive the news that he had successful surgery and would make a full recovery. Now the bad news – this individual had no health insurance and no means to pay the massive medical bills he incurred. Most of you could share similar stories where a friend or family member's life was substantially impacted by a serious health issue or cost of care.

As president of a company employing over 275 individuals, I know the power of health care. Finding the right balance between a multi-million dollar expense and the best care options for your employees and their families is a major challenge – one that requires expertise for employers and individuals to navigate.

Jon Warner has provided that guidance to countless companies and their employees for almost 30 years. Following 14 years in the insurance industry, Jon started his business, JP Warner Associates, Inc., in 1997 to service companies' employee benefit needs. He has been a leader and champion of Consumer Driven Health Plans and creative plan designs.

Jon has a unique ability to sift through the deluge of ever-changing health care legislation and trendy acronyms to provide real world meaning in layman's terms. He does so with the perspective of someone deeply rooted in faith who always remembers behind every medical expense there is a life being impacted.

Jon and I share a very personal connection to this topic. Both Jon and my mother had successful life-saving surgery performed by the same surgeon at Jefferson University Hospital in Philadelphia. They were both blessed to have access and financial means to get the best care options available in the world.

Whether you are a business owner, manager, hourly worker, or unemployed victim of the recession, you can benefit from the guidance provided in this book. Serious health conditions do not discriminate and when they occur, we all want to be in a position to get the best care for ourselves and our families.

How to Win the Health Care Game provides background on how our current health care system evolved and choices you can make to get the best care at a price and risk tolerance unique to your situation. You will finish this book with an understanding of Consumer Driven Health Plans, Wellness programs and the powerful impact they can have on your physical and financial well being.

We face significant changes in our health care system due to the PPACA legislation, also known as the Affordable Care Act and Obamacare. I tell our employees openly that I do not have a perfect solution to eliminate rising medical expenses, nor does the government; however, I strongly believe in Jon Warner's premise that an educated medical consumer with financial ownership will make better decisions for themselves and their family than executives and politicians.

Kirk A. Putt
President & CEO R-V Industries, Inc.

Dedicated to the memory of **Edwin T. Johnson,** (1930 – 2012), founder and CEO of The Johnson Companies, Newtown, PA. Ed's confidence has inspired many fellow Americans to plan for their future.

Background for Winning the Health Care Game

I. The Winner's Approach to Health Insurance Protection

A winning strategy is catching on to best afford highly desirable, yet expensive American health care. The change that is taking hold across America includes accepting short term risk to free up dollars that allow for longer term savings. This will win the health care game.

The truth is that most people have an inconsistent need for high cost health care, and yet we define excellent health insurance as coverage that minimizes how much we must spend out of our pockets when we need care. The best coverage has the highest premium and pre-pays for regular, reoccurring medical service and product needs plus expensive care to protect our financial well-being.

We are easily swayed to justify spending more on health insurance because it is complicated when sorting out value. It is also hard to learn and re-learn how it is supposed to work, and a challenge to gauge realistic financial risk. Charges for services can be so much greater than discounts. Questions arise about what should be and is covered. And since so many of us only use health insurance some of the time, it adds to peace of mind to buy an expensive plan and hope for the best.

We live during a time of incredible and expensive medical miracles and think about the advances yet to come! Since so many of us only use health insurance some of the time it is a challenge to gauge realistically how much financial risk makes sense to assume now, and what we should be saving for the future. While easier if all expenses are paid in full at time of need, this is not necessarily smart.

Even though our inconsistent need for high cost care seems like it cannot be well quantified or communicated due to life's risks, winners are looking long term and embracing a new way of thinking about maintaining health insurance that will pay for high cost needs and paying for normal care needs with premium savings.

ANNUAL FREQUENCY OF HEALTH CARE SERVICES

- **60% of us use normal health care services such as Office visits & Rx**
- **15% of us incur no health care costs**
- **25% of us require high cost health care such as Hospitalization, Surgery, X-ray & Laboratory services**

It was only 100 years ago that most people passed away before they reached age 60. Today, 60 is the new age 40 with many of us anticipating living into our 90's or even to 100! Life extending research coupled with health improving technologies, procedures, products and services available is amazing compared with even one generation ago.

Skyrocketing costs have accompanied health care progress, so it should be of little surprise the American government has moved to regulate our growing use of health care resources. The laudable goal exists that all Americans, regardless of financial means have access to the latest and best technology. It has turned into the largest legislative mandate of the 21st century.

The opportunity continues to exist for most of us to have 100% of our future health care needs paid in full in order to win the health care game. It comes down building equity while accepting reasonable risk.

Concern always exists that we may be diagnosed with a life threatening condition caused by illness or an accident. Our lifestyle choices while younger become habits that add to anticipation about expensive health care problems later on in life. And as our body's age, pains increase our need and desire for medical services to enhance quality of life.

There are great grandparents alive today thanks to health care advances who were born at home before hospitals offered maternity services, and before health insurance was created. Americans benefit daily now due to artificial joint and valve replacements and even organ transplants. Thousands of new medicines have been perfected in recent times. Saving lives and extending life span is a great success story of this modern era. Savings for future health care needs yet to be discovered is the winning strategy. Since advances are likely to cost more and more, turn now to pages 111 & 112 for savings examples that will allow you to be prepared.

The Affordable Care Act, also known as PPACA (Patient Protection & Affordable Care Act) and Obamacare simplify how much risk to assume and premium to pay upfront for health insurance. One's choice of "precious metal" or "metallic" plan will come with varying levels of cash flow responsibility. The lower the premium the greater the cash flow responsibility before health insurance begins to pay.

Under The Affordable Care Act "Platinum, Gold, Silver and Bronze" health insurance plans incrementally reduce or increase out of pocket cost exposure. All government authorized health insurance plans must cover an unlimited amount of high cost care, so risk acceptance becomes a personal decision about how much to spend upfront in premium.

Americans appreciate the convenience of having normal health care needs paid for by health insurance.

And yet, since less than half of us actively use our coverage at any one time, awareness is building that the Platinum Plan standard which includes pre-paying for all of our normal care needs is financially inefficient.

Marketplace reality is coming quickly that more and more Americans will make insurance plan selections after comparing the "full premium cost", that being 100% of the premium. Currently health insurance premium awareness for many is limited to payroll deductions representing a minority percentage of the real cost. A shift in our sense of value occurs once the total premium cost becomes known. Platinum plan selection with mostly 100% coverage can be thousands of dollars more in premium than quality alternatives.

Can it be excellent health insurance no longer costs the most premium? Although this sounds contrarian, it has been proven over the past ten years that this is true. Accepting the challenge to convincingly back up this thesis means navigating the new health insurance landscape with a longer term perspective.

Pre-tax account options increase the attraction of insurance coverage that includes neutralizing out of pocket cost exposure using:

- **Health Savings Accounts**
- **Flexible Spending Accounts**
- **Health Reimbursement Arrangements**

The 50 year old couple who is disappointed about inferior coverage today versus 20 years ago when they gave birth to a child for $5 is likely not fully aware of premium cost increases over time and efficient options that include pre-tax savings accounts now available.

Many societal advances catch on because they reduce risk, although it is never completely eliminated. Bringing along an umbrella, raincoat and boots on a day when the forecast calls for heavy downpours is prudent. When the forecast calls for occasional showers and may mean you get wet, lugging along extra gear to avoid the risk is usually not worth it. Being educated about life's opportunities and trade-offs includes insurance selection.

Adding to this rationale is a truism about having some skin in the game to impact decision making. **Milton Friedman** will always be remembered as a brilliant economist. He summarized well why health insurance should include a reasonable amount personal out of pocket risk: "No one spends someone else's money as carefully as their own."

"No one
spends
someone else's
money as
carefully as
their own."

II. Health Insurance History

Many Americans with limited income remain uninsured because it is too costly. At the same time, many of us are inefficiently over-insured.

The history of America's private and public health insurance system is less than 100 years old, dating back to the 1930's with the introduction of hospitalization insurance coverage. To stabilize revenue and to grow, hospitals banded together to form <u>Hospital Service Plans</u>. Using the concept of insurance, a nominal premium was charged to many individuals, guaranteeing 100% payment for inpatient care for a certain number of days if ever needed. By spreading the cost of care to a large group, individual citizens paid a small premium, which covered the expense of the ever-changing five percent of the population whose health care needs require expensive treatment in a hospital setting.

Hospital Service Plans, which were rebranded as Blue Cross Plans, took time to catch on. They received an enrollment boost in the 1940's as employers agreed to pay premiums for their workers to enhance compensation during the wage and price control period necessitated by World War II. Tax deductible employer paid hospitalization insurance premiums soon became an accepted cost of business for employers and a valued benefit to employees and family members.

In the 1950's as more sophisticated and specialized physician care became available, Blue Shield plans commenced spreading risk and achieving affordability for in-patient doctor's services. By design, Blue Cross and Blue Shield plans paid 100% of the cost of care for a limited number of days of service. Since available services were limited, premiums were relatively affordable. Surgeons were the busiest in hospitals then, extracting and correcting problems with scalpel and suture. Many inpatient and outpatient health care treatment approaches available today were unknown then.

With the addition of Major Medical coverage in the 1960's, comprehensive insurance coverage for office visits and prescriptions became available. These Major Medical plans required satisfaction of a deductible, followed by the requirement to pay 20% of the cost of care. This established a basis for cost sharing to keep premiums from quickly rising. It also made sense due to the high utilization of these normal, reoccurring health care needs.

Major Medical plans were marketed and sold by for-profit insurers. Over time these companies developed their own comprehensive health insurance products and began competing with regional Blue Cross and Blue Shield plans. The for profit insurer's national administrative reach often better served multi-site employers.

Prior to The Affordable Care Act, health care legislation's greatest impact on our citizenry began with the passage of Medicare for seniors in 1964, followed by Medicaid for the impoverished. Those suffering from certain chronic illnesses such as kidney failure became eligible for Medicare even if not of retirement age. The Health Maintenance Organization (HMO) Act became law in 1973 for the under age 65 population.

Medicare Parts A & B today include deductibles and coinsurance, covering a limited number of treatment days. Medicare Part A hospitalization benefits reduce in value after 60 days inpatient, and are exhausted after 150 days of inpatient care. This may seem barbaric in the 21st Century, but back in the 1960's this standard was used to limit the government's risk and was better than nothing.

In contrast, HMOs were originally designed to include an unlimited number of days of coverage and evolved to be known as "Managed Care" which ended up as code for "limiting" expensive care availability.

The HMO Act of 1973 promulgated a pre-payment system to providers of care so they accepted liability for managing reoccurring health care needs. HMOs originally eliminated deductibles and coinsurance in favor of nominal, flat copays per visit. HMOs established contractual relationships with hospitals and doctors to share risk in the treatment of patients.

HMO plans also included preventive care services to promote good health. They contrasted with traditional insurance plans that were truly "sick insurance" plans, offering payments only if a diagnosis confirmed an illness or accident.

Copay plans formed the basis of the late 20th century "Managed Care" era. HMOs (Health Maintenance Organizations), PPOs (Preferred Provider Organizations) and POS (Point of Service) plans dominated. Multi-year pre-payment contracts with hospital and physician providers successfully minimized premium increases and out-of-pocket responsibility. Reductions in personal, out of pocket responsibility for health care became the new standard. A generation of Americans grew up used to paying very little out of pocket when accessing health care services. It was a Nirvana period for the well insured.

America's aging population and the ever increasing number of available and government mandated health care services ultimately led to year upon year of double digit percentage premium cost escalation. This prompted employers to charge employees increasingly higher amounts from paychecks in order to maintain health coverage.

With premium rates ever increasing, new thinking occurred about how much pre-paid health coverage is efficient. As deductibles and out of pocket responsibility increased, in 2002 rules were released allowing employers to offer a <u>Health Reimbursement Arrangement</u> (HRA) to limit personal cost exposure. Many employers use HRAs to reimburse a portion of qualified health care expenses that are not paid by insurance plans.

Legislation signed at the end of 2003 that introduced prescription coverage for seniors also included language introducing Health Savings Accounts (HSA). These are pre-tax savings plans similar to Individual Retirement Accounts (IRA), and are eligible to participants enrolled in government approved High Deductible Health Plan (HDHP) designs.

Flexible Spending Accounts (FSA), first enacted in 1978 were enhanced in 2005 and 2006 with the addition of Over-The-Counter (OTC) products and therapies available for reimbursement on a pre-tax basis. Although somewhat reduced in value with The Affordable Care Act, the two and a half month extension to use up FSA unspent balances continues to minimize concerns about the "Use it or Lose it Rule", ensuring ongoing popularity for these voluntary plans.

Employers who have embraced HSAs, HRAs and FSAs lower health care premiums with the goal of maintaining or reducing out of pocket cost responsibility. While this is a different coverage approach than what many became accustomed to during the Managed Care era, growing acceptance of HSAs, HRAs and FSAs continues as a logical and efficient way to limit premium increases. Catastrophic insurance protection coupled with options to pay out of pocket costs on a pre-tax basis is the most efficient way to win the health care game.

Health Plan Design
Continuum

1930s	1973	1980s	1990s	2002	2004
Traditional Indemnity *Insurance*	**HMO** *Coverage*	**PPO** *Coverage*	**POS** *Coverage*	Consumer Driven Health Plan (HRA) *Coverage & Insurance*	High Deductible Health Plan (HSA) *Insurance*

III. Inefficient Copays vs. Deductibles

Full coverage health plans are priced to minimize out-of-pocket expenses so that the cost to see a doctor should not rationalize avoidance of medical treatment. Here is an example. You slice open your finger while preparing for your family dinner. "What is that doctor going to do anyway if there is no need for stitches and just a lot of blood?" Well, what if you have not received a tetanus shot in a long time and maybe the wound is deep enough for stitches and just maybe you did not clean it well and it becomes infected?

If you are paying 100% of the bill and money is tight, you may accept the risk of greater sickness and disability. Or, so the theory goes, if you have a nominal copay of $20 to $40 for a visit to an urgent care center, then you will receive professional care immediately. An emergency room visit is excluded from this example as even copay plans require $100 to $200 and this need is better attended to elsewhere.

Since premium costs are tax deductible to employers, historical tendencies have been to select pre-paid coverage plans that include normal care needs like attending to wounds, with the peace of mind knowing what is provide is "the best coverage available". Full coverage health plans in theory eliminate barriers for receiving all the care a patient and their doctor thinks they need.

Unfortunately over time, ever higher premium rates emerge to pay for:

1. Excess Utilization - Minimal personal cost responsibility too often translates to redundant and higher cost health care usage. Economic concerns are minimized in the spirit of taking advantage of all available treatment and recovery options.

2. Administrative Overhead - Think about it in terms of percentages. The insurance company adds 15% - 20% above projected claim expenses for claims processing, risk acceptance, profit, commissions and government taxes both state and federal now that can add another 5%. Insurance companies and the government generate the most money from full coverage plans.

3. Hyper inflated Charges - Confusion caused by the difference between charges and discounts, plus billing errors add to cost but are someone else's concern when 100% of care is paid in full.

Paying flat copays ($20, $40, $100) per health care service event is the standard in today's traditional health plans. Copays are convenient.

Although it is unusual in our free market economy to make a purchase without regard to its cost, this occurs when patient responsibility is limited to copays, as they mask the real cost of health care services. Well-intentioned plan designers accomplished this cost sharing approach in the 1980's & 1990's, replacing deductibles and coinsurance as the new standard. We had it all with affordable, tax deductible premiums and quality care available instantly at time of need for a nominal out of pocket cost.

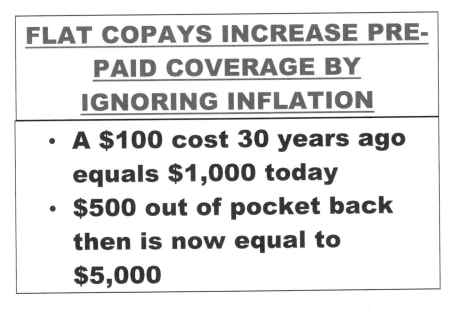

FLAT COPAYS INCREASE PRE-PAID COVERAGE BY IGNORING INFLATION

- **A $100 cost 30 years ago equals $1,000 today**
- **$500 out of pocket back then is now equal to $5,000**

As health premium increases outpace inflation year after year, advocates of cost efficiency have considered whether copays are the appropriate mechanism for cost sharing. Before HMOs, PPOs, & POS plans, health insurance included deductibles and coinsurance. Deductible levels increased over time and coinsurance responsibility averaged 20% of the cost of the care received up to an out-of-pocket limit, followed by 100% protection for high cost care needs.

Lower premiums are charged for plans that include deductibles and coinsurance versus copay plans, as

risk is transferred to the patient. Cost awareness increases the patient's sense of value and selection.

Being open to a reasonable level of risk acceptance achieves lower premium costs. Since 11% of our population is hospitalized each year, coverage for this type of protection merits including risk acceptance since usage is limited. And yet, since a hospital experience can result in many thousands of dollars in cost it may seem counter intuitive to accept financial risk for such a circumstance. Getting practical and thinking about how many days you have been a hospital inpatient as compared to the days you have been alive helps with philosophical acceptance. How often do we carry an umbrella when the chance of rain is 11%?

A traditional way to temper premium increases while keeping patients in touch with the cost of health care is the acceptance of coinsurance. After a deductible is satisfied, insurance pays 70% to 90% of costs to an "out of pocket" maximum. It's important to grasp the out-of-pocket cap, where 90% or 80% or 70% in coverage transitions to 100% coverage.

Consider over the course of your lifetime how often personal or family health care expenses have reached $50,000 in a year. With 10% coinsurance to this amount, one accepts $5,000 in out of pocket risk. With The Affordable Care Act a single person's maximum out of pocket exposure is $6,350 in 2014. A plan with a $1,500 deductible and 10% coinsurance to the maximum out of pocket allowed by law transitions to

100% coverage once annual covered expenses exceed $50,000. Sorry if confusing but remember that all health insurance plans will pay 100% of costs eventually. And of course the lowest cost way to pay out of pocket expenses is on a pre-tax basis.

"DRIP" VERSUS "GUSHER" MENTALITY

Protection from an unaffordable financial health care cost "Gusher" is the most important reason to be insured. Minimizing personal cost responsibility with plans that have low copays is based on a premise that too few Americans have emergency resources.

Consider the example of being responsible for the first $2,000 of cost if admitted to the hospital. While this is a lot of money if living from paycheck to paycheck, consider how it compares financially to the cost of smoking a pack of cigarettes per day. Pack a day smokers spend more than $2,000 per year once addicted to this costly and deadly habit.

It is intriguing how we place a different financial value on "Gusher" risk versus the daily purchase of "death sticks", which include cigarettes and salty high fat foods like greasy French fries. To reinforce the point, the cost to buy lunch at fast food restaurants now averages around $8 per meal. If purchased every work day over 50 weeks, that annual outlay is $2,000.

In America we culturally support a "Drip Mentality" approach to cash flow. Our drip deductions from gross earnings can be so significant that we learn to live on a net amount that is up to 50% less than full pay when including taxes, insurance and retirement savings payroll deductions.

DRIP VS GUSHER LINKAGE

Why not Drip your own money into a Health Savings Account so you have emergency funds when Gusher health care costs occur? This is more efficient than paying a higher premium for a lower out of pocket cost exposure now. Remember that HSA funds are _your_ money! (See pages 111 & 112)

Since most paychecks are reduced to pay a portion of health insurance premiums, assessing copay versus deductible and coinsurance coverage plans is prudent and increasingly common. Winning the health care game requires studying the value of the convenience of low copays for services that mask the true cost of care.

IV. Obamacare Fulfills a Promise

Healthy citizens add to our country's competitive edge in the global market place. Workers are most productive when they feel well. This is not discussed often enough by business leaders as a reason why health insurance is offered as a benefit to employees. Park your pre-conceived notions about Obamacare and think objectively about these questions:

1. Should employers who do not invest in the health care needs of their workers be required to pay into a fund to assist their employees to purchase their own health insurance protection?

2. Should part time workers, the disabled and retirees have access to the same level of insurance protection as fulltime workers?

3. Since many purchases occur today utilizing the power of the Internet, why not health insurance?

Long term planners foresee a time when all Americans will go online to select a health insurance plan of their choice. Prices will be based upon age, income and the amount of pre-paid services built into the coverage. Private insurance companies will accept all applicants regardless of their health history. Business owners, union leaders, financial and human resource executives will no longer decide on plan choices. Employers and employees will no longer look at health insurance as an unpredictable budget item.

This may come true as the foundation for such a development has been rolling out since President Barack Obama signed legislation that was voted for along Democratic Party lines to massively change the American health care system. The well-intentioned goal of uniform health insurance coverage for all Americans finally, after many attempts spanning decades, culminated in 2010 when the Patient Protection & Affordable Care Act (PPACA) became law.

The framework for personalized health insurance purchase along with tighter quality of care by hospitals and doctors will hopefully serve future generations of Americans well. Long overdue insurance rules in the law require acceptance by an insurer if pre-existing medical conditions exist, plus offer parents' the ability to insure children until age 26. Unlimited payments to allow the chronically ill to never exhaust their overall financial resources plus 100% preventive care coverage add to this comprehensive law. The annual out of pocket cost maximum per individual and family before insurance must pay 100% is well thought out, along with health care marketplace exchange options that offer subsidies to maintain insurance post-employment.

Since the uninsured cost of spending more than a day in the hospital can equal the price of a new automobile and result in personal bankruptcy, these are welcome protections. It is all great if affordable and not overly bureaucratic.

A GARGANTUAN CHALLENGE

Obamacare includes new taxes, reduces Medicare spending and expands government oversight, plus introduces penalties for those opting not to be insured. Employers not offering insurance to full-time workers must pay into a fund to help subsidize their workers individual purchase of insurance. These are well publicized, gargantuan challenges to the success of the legislation, so significant to merit a Supreme Court ruling.

Most Americans have become used to having the health care services paid mostly in full with access to care instantly available. The expectation of full coverage started with the HMO Act of 1973, which set a framework for low cost health coverage that included nominal copays for office visits, tests, prescriptions and even expensive hospitalization. Nirvana was achieved for about ten years in the 1980's and 1990's combining low out of pocket, pre-paid insurance protection with affordable premiums.

HMO plans began falling out of favor though due to patient complaints about being turned down for desired services. Doctors and hospitals complained that HMOs excessively denied approval for recommended care. Lawsuits and bad press focused on insurance companies who manage and sell HMO plans. The HMOs and insurers became the bad guys.

The Affordable Care Act is similar to the HMO approach for managing appropriate care and

denying coverage for certain services, except this time Accountable Care Organizations (ACOs), the new term for hospital and physician groups are financially motivated to monitor the amount of health care provided. The law penalizes providers for not maintaining cost efficiency standards.

This change may lead to increased waiting lists and more litigation if supply restrictions do not keep pace with patient demands. The law addresses health care delivery standardization, for better or the opposite. Optimistic proponents argue the incentives and disincentives in The Affordable Care Act increase efficiency while maintaining quality standards and reducing costs. Time will tell if this new thinking is in everyone's best interests.

The law achieves many laudable goals and yet does not address:

1. Lawsuit (tort) reform to reduce defensive testing by physicians concerned with accusations of malpractice.
2. Excessive hospital and physician charges.
3. Lack of consumer price awareness between competing hospital and physician practices.

Some argue that expanded awareness by patients of the cost and value of recommended care will not help to lower costs. Leave it to the health care professionals to choose what care to deliver and the lawyers and judges to sort out who is at fault when problems occur. Others believe better education about costs and functionality may motivate a higher percentage of Americans to take better care of ourselves and lowering costs.

Health care consumption begins when patients seek care and treatment for accidents, illnesses and diseases. Physicians sign orders for every diagnostic health care dollar that is spent. Changing payment standards and incentives is a welcome part of The Affordable Care Act, transitioning from fee for service to bundled payments to providers of care for restoring patient health. The hospitals and doctors have no choice but to bear increased financial and quality risk.

HEALTH INSURANCE FOR ALL
A primary goal of The Affordable Care Act is to add 30 million more Americans to health insurance rolls as a form of social justice. Questions include whether all Americans benefit from this expansion as it will challenge physician and hospital resources. One concern is that the newly insured may strain the system because of a spike in demand for medical services. The maturation of PPACA raises many questions:

- Have increased utilization projections for the newly insured been properly accounted for?
- Will there be enough physicians and support personnel to provide quality services?
- Are comprehensive insurance coverage levels overly generous, resulting in unaffordable premiums even with subsidies?

- Will new regulatory restrictions on health insurance companies allow proper rate setting to cover added costs?
- Are additional tax increases inevitable to subsidize the true cost of expanded coverage?

Under The Affordable Care Act the maximum payroll deduction allowed for workers is 9.5% of pay. If you earn $40,000 per year, the cap is $3,800 or $146 per bi-weekly pay. That is a high amount to charge!

The high cost of health insurance is becoming better known due to the law, shocking many at just how expensive it is to be well insured. As full premiums become known, an increased acceptance of risk before insurance kicks in is inevitable to maintain premium affordability.

PENALTY TAX TOO LOW

It may surprise you that 75% of us do not incur substantial health care costs each year. This truth challenges compliance with The Affordable Care Act for many Americans who are supposed to voluntarily purchase coverage on Health Care Exchanges. It is much more expensive to purchase subsidized health coverage than to accept the Penalty Tax for not buying insurance.

In 2016, a couple earning $40,000 will likely be able to purchase a mid-level Silver plan for about $200 per month, or $2,400 annually once the government subsidy is subtracted from the true premium cost. Their

Penalty Tax is $500 in 2014, $1,000 in 2015 and caps out at $1,390, or 58% of subsidized premiums in 2016. Since the plan available at this premium amount will include deductibles and copays, remaining uninsured may appear more attractive assuming the couple rarely uses health care services.

The PPACA law does not allow wage garnishment or the ability to place a lien on personal property to collect the Penalty Tax. The Penalty Tax is collected by reducing Annual Federal Income Tax Refund amounts.

The Penalty Tax for being uninsured is collected annually at tax time, versus health insurance premiums that must be paid each month. Think about what you would do when premium costs compete with paying for food and rent. And the law includes nine hardship exceptions allowing the Penalty Tax to be waived. So, even though subsidized, health insurance purchases by the healthy may continue to be an unaffordable luxury.

Because voluntary participation by healthier individuals will likely fall short, health care marketplace exchange enrollment is destined to be lower than adequate, and claims costs higher than hoped for. Since health insurance must now pay for all pre-existing medical conditions, the ill will sign up knowing their care needs are greater than the premium they will pay, and as time passes those who go from being healthy to sick will then enroll when they anticipate spending more in claims than their personal cost for premiums.

Insurance only works if premiums paid in are greater than claims costs going out. As premiums rise for the sick people who buy insurance, even the marginally ill may opt out, putting pressure on the government to legislate additional taxes to cover the shortfall.

It is a wonder why the Penalty Tax became such a lightning bolt issue, rising to the U.S. Supreme Court to affirm its validity when Medicare uses a proven approach to maximize voluntarily participation. The Medicare penalty is effective because if you do not sign up for insurance when first eligible your premiums include a surcharge when enrolled later. It costs more to delay. A future penalty approach including late enrollment surcharges similar to Medicare, with caps on how much the premium may increase, is a worthy alternative to the current Penalty Tax.

With all of these observations, both positive and critical, applaud that for the first time in America a worker who gets sick or hurt and loses their job can continue to be insured for health care needs at a reasonable cost. This is a wonderful expression of our compassionate society, and if establishing a health care savings fund while healthy emerges as an expected personal responsibility, this will enhance long term health insurance affordability for all.

"THE AFFORDABLE CARE ACT"

Obamacare is a wealth redistribution law. It makes expensive health care affordable for Americans not fortunate enough to have subsidized health insurance coverage through employment. All Americans with employer provided insurance share in the wealth redistribution cost by paying fees & taxes built into premiums. In addition, higher income earners pay more in personal income taxes allowing lower income individuals to purchase financially subsidized insurance from health care marketplace exchanges.

V. <u>Alphabet Soup – HSA, FSA & HRA</u>

Americans with an inconsistent need for health care services are taught to purchase insurance anticipating near term catastrophe. The Affordable Care Act is unfortunately silent on personal savings for future health care needs. Fortunately it did little to change legislation passed in 2003 introducing Health Savings Accounts.

Plan designs named for precious metals promote nominal out of pocket insurance protection using terms like Platinum and Gold. This continues a tradition of "renting" high cost health insurance protection as the standard, even though costly and inefficient. While counter intuitive that first dollar protection is merited for most of us, the law promotes such a philosophy.

The winner's paradigm change gaining momentum includes accepting reasonable insurance risk while building a tax preferred fund for future health care needs. Implementing a savings strategy in your 40s is likely to result in savings values of $100,000+ by retirement age. Adopting a personal health care retirement savings philosophy allows building equity similar to savings in 401k and 403b retirement savings plans. Consider again pages 111 & 112.

The high deductible cash flow risk for health care costs before insurance coverage takes over can be neutralized using HSAs or FSAs and HRAs. There is some lighthearted history worthy of comment as it relates to the original introduction of pre-tax accounts to pay for health care out of pocket health care expenses.

FSAs (Flexible Spending Accounts) initially became available more than 30 years ago. Back then touch tone telephone # & * functions only worked in laboratories and at Disney's Future World. Computer screens emitted a green hue and were typically found in basement laboratories. Personal computing including hand held devices that we take for granted today were science fiction. Professors accepted handwritten papers to complete most assignments, so even typing had limited value for college students. If one's thesis required typing it might be completed by a professor's spouse for a few cents per word.

This was the 1970's, a bellwether period in employee benefits regulation, mostly focused on retirement plans. The Employee Retiree Income Security Act (ERISA) became law in 1974, followed by popular retirement and health premium savings pre-tax programs, Section 401k, Section 403b and Section 125, outlined in the 1978 Revenue Act.

Section 125 validated a "Flexible Compensation" approach referred to as the Cafeteria Plan. Think about picking up a tray and choosing between a ham & cheese on rye versus the turkey platter. Compare this to employees choosing from a menu of benefit options including medical, dental and life insurance, paying for purchases with financial "credit dollars" provided by their employer. Spend more than the employer offers in credits, and voluntary personal, pre-tax payroll deductions make up the difference.

The return to Cafeteria type benefit plans is an outgrowth of The Affordable Care Act. Private Exchange Defined Contribution insurance approaches that expose full premium value are increasing in popularity, educating us to know how much health insurance options really cost. This trend is a consequence of the creation of health insurance marketplace exchanges and a logical outgrowth with insurance premiums now listed on annual Form W-2 summary of earnings.

Starting in 2018 The Affordable Care Act includes the collection of 40% excise taxes on premiums exceeding a threshold amount, called the Cadillac tax. This increased awareness of how much pre-paid insurance to buy and risk to assume before health insurance starts to pay is moving to the forefront acceptance of qualified High Deductible Health Plans (HDHP).

HEALTH SAVINGS ACCOUNTS (HSA)
Every year since their creation late in 2003, the number of Americans with HSAs has increased. In 2012 alone, HSA accounts grew 22%. Appreciation and acceptance of HSAs requires a paradigm shift from "renting" insurance protection versus coverage protection that builds "equity and ownership." Building a Health Savings Account is fundamental to winning the health care game.

You have likely heard about HSAs but maybe never dug into why people set them up. Once it is clarified that Health Savings Accounts (HSA) may only be funded if enrolled in a federally qualified High Deductible Health Plan (HDHP), some lose interest. Another challenge is that since they are "savings" accounts, the build-up of funds generally occurs over time. HSAs protect cash flow only after there are adequate funds saved in the account. Pre-tax deposit amounts to HSAs are also capped annually.

Navigating towards the most cost efficient health insurance coverage in the age of health care reform still means more and more Americans are jumping over these hurdles and setting up HSAs. These accounts are destined to become the fourth leg of a sound retirement plan.

FOURTH LEG OF THE RETIREMENT STOOL

1. Social Security
2. Retirement Plan Savings
3. Personal Savings including equity in a home
4. Health Savings Account

High Deductible Health Plan (HDHP) enrollment is required to fund an HSA. HDHPs on first impression are not considered "good coverage" because of their low premium cost and all diagnostic services subject to satisfaction of an upfront deductible. Nothing is paid by the insurance company for normal care needs.

And yet, coupled with premium savings deposited into an HSA to pay for normal care expenses, the combination offers better long term protection. Since most of us have an inconsistent need for expensive health care services, combining low cost premiums with pre-tax savings for future health care costs allows for building an account that eliminates cash flow risk.

The deductible and coinsurance layer of patient financial responsibility also prompts scrutinization of the cost and value of health care purchases. While maximizing awareness of the real cost of health care services, it is most appreciated by accounting oriented consumers, while confusing and frustrating to others.

The entire discounted cost of sickness related office visits and prescriptions are subject to the HDHP deductible. Services are "covered", but the insurance does not "pay" until the deductible has been met.

A fundamental premise of an HDHP is to replace copays that mask the true cost of health care services with deductibles ranging from $1,500 to $5,000 for individuals, and $3,000 to $10,000 for two or more covered family members. Deductibles generally double for coverage that includes dependents. The family deductible is "aggregate", which means that one or multiple family members may accumulate expenses to satisfy the entire deductible. All but preventive care services accumulate towards satisfying the deductible.

Once deductible amounts are paid out, plans cover 100%, 90%, 80% or 70% of additional medical expenses until the participant reaches a final threshold, or "annual out of pocket" maximum. At that time the HDHP insurance plan pays 100% of covered health care costs for the balance of the plan year. HDHPs include 100% coverage for expensive, catastrophic health care costs, as do all Obamacare approved plans.

HDHP participants have the option of opening a personally owned Health Savings Account (HSA). Deposits to the account are not taxed as income. HSA funds may be invested to earn interest that is not taxed, and unused balances roll over to future years. HSA account owners have the opportunity to build savings to offset future health care out-of-pocket costs. While there are limits to the amount of money that may be deposited annually into an HSA, there is no cap on lifetime HSA savings.

Employers may deposit funds into employee HSAs to reduce deductible and out-of-pocket risk. For money to be deposited into an HSA, an individual must be insured only by an HDHP. It is important to maintain the context that rules and restrictions regarding tax savings in this arrangement focus on pre-tax Health Savings Accounts (HSAs).

Legally it is possible for an individual to be covered under an HDHP and a traditional health plan at the same time. If this is the case though, they may not deposit pre-tax funds into an HSA. HRAs and FSAs, reviewed in detail in the next section may be used instead of HSAs to limit out of pocket exposure, but may not be used in tandem with funding HSAs to pay for medical and prescription expenses until the deductible has been paid in full.

Think about HSAs as having exclusivity rules. They must stand on their own. The positives are striking:

1. Deposits are not taxed as income.
2. HSA money is the property of the account owner.
3. HSA accounts are portable if changing jobs or retiring.
4. Upon death funds pass to a beneficiary.

Rules enhancing the flexibility and value of Health Savings Accounts were released in 2007. These clarifications advanced opportunities for HSA account owners to save more money on a pre-tax basis for post-retirement health care expenses.

Adjustments included:

A. Allowing annual deposits up to $1,000 as a catch up provision for participants age 55 until enrolled in Medicare.

B. The "Last Month" rule allowing a full year tax deduction for HSA money deposited at any time during the calendar year until April 15 of the following year, assuming the participant maintains HDHP coverage.

C. Account holders may add funds up to the legal annual maximum to reimburse themselves for care incurred if an existing HSA balance is less than the amount of health care expenses incurred the date care was received. HDHP coverage must continue for 12 months following such deposits to avoid penalties.

D. Employers have the option to deposit more money into an HSA for lower paid personnel than highly compensated employees.

E. Individual IRA transfers are allowed once per lifetime into an HSA. This opportunity negates having to pay taxes in the future on IRA savings used for qualified health care expenses.

Regardless of one's age, payments from an HSA avoid taxation and penalties if used for federally qualified health expenses under Section 213d, plus for Medicare Advantage Plan premiums and for Long Term Care insurance. HSA money is never taxed if used to pay for qualified health care expenses. What is not spent in a year earns tax-free interest and rolls over to the next year. Income, interest, and distribution taxation are avoided.

Prior to age 65, if HSA deposits are used to pay for purchases other than qualified health expenses, the account owner is responsible to pay a 20% penalty along with income taxes. Post age 65 there is no longer a penalty spending savings on non-health care purchases. If used for normal retirement needs income taxes then apply. Upon death, unspent HSA money is passed to a chosen beneficiary who is afforded the same tax treatment available to the original account holder.

HSAs are offered with a Debit Card to pay for health care services. Personally maintaining receipts for six years is required by law if ever audited. Third party substantiation of expenditures is not required. Self-management adds to the value of HSAs.

COMMITMENT CONTRACT
There is a way to design an HDHP and HSA by increasing payroll deductions. Presenting two or three payroll deduction options that include additional Health Savings Account funding engages people to consider

HSAs. "Commitment Contracts" which are forced savings plans, allow price point comparison with higher cost HMO and PPO plans.

Proper disclosure is paramount to the Commitment Contract strategy. Questions and comments may arise that an employer is not "giving up anything" by offering higher payroll deductions to fund an HSA at an increased level. Value enhancement will definitely occur if an employer pre-funds 50% or more of the annual HSA amount at the beginning of the plan year. The point is that HDHP and HSA plans may be offered with multiple contribution levels.

Since additional payroll deduction amounts are voluntary they may be adjusted up or down during the year. This approach maximizes flexibility as individuals may suspend their HSA contributions if other financial responsibilities arise during the year.

HDHP METALLIC PLAN COMPARISON

Platinum – HSA Funded to IRS max
Gold – HSA Funded to 80% of the deductible
Silver – HSA Funded to 60% of the deductible
Bronze – No HSA Funding

HSA deposits will grow and roll over after a year or two of forced savings for infrequent users of high cost health care services. Future deductible and out of pocket risk is then eliminated. Accepting risk has a limited time horizon.

Dr. Benjamin Carson, the featured speaker at the 2013 National Prayer Breakfast attended by President and Mrs. Obama spoke on a broad range of topics including health care efficiency. His primary recommendation in addition to providing a birth certificate to newborn babies is to set up:

1. An Electronic Medical Record
2. A Pre-tax Health Savings Account

Why? As he stated, the elderly person with six diseases will consider differently whether to spend all of those savings for life extension versus passing along that money to loved ones. In addition, patients will learn to be responsible about costs when they seek health care services, versus running to the emergency room for care that is not life threatening.

While considered controversial comments to some, by having the financial means to consider health care decisions, more efficient choices will occur regardless of income.

Here is a realistic Health Savings Account example. Let's say you are purchasing health insurance for yourself and your family. Your deductible is $5,000 and your employer funds the first $2,000 of your HSA. You anticipate spending $2,500 on family health care needs in a typical year. If you fund an additional $3,000 into your HSA the net amount pre-tax equivalent deducted per bi-weekly pay is about $80. At the end of your first year $2,500 will be saved. When your employer funds

$2,000 the following year, you now have $4,500 to spend. If you continue with the same voluntary $3,000 deduction and your family has the same $2,000 in costs, your account balance is $5,000 plus pre-tax interest at year end. A cushion has been built and you are on your way to building the fourth leg of the retirement stool.

COMPARISON TO COPAY PLANS
Although upfront deductible plans continue to grow in popularity, employers offering multiple health insurance options often see a majority of participants selecting higher cost plans with copays. Since health care needs are inconsistent and perceived value is often limited to the comparative price tag or payroll deduction amount, selecting the "best" coverage is believed by the less educated means selecting the highest price plan. While we desire to minimize out-of-pocket costs throughout the year, the added cost of convenience is so high it results from being ill informed and resistant to change.

In an HMO, POS or PPO plan with copays, if a specialist doctor's office visit costs $150, it may be that a patient's copay for the appointment is $50. The insurance company then forwards $100 to complete the transaction. The insurer, as allowed by the PPACA law, includes a $15 or $20 processing fee in premiums charged on top of the $100 paid to the doctor. The same convenience surcharge is tacked onto a $150 prescription. An average 2% state tax plus The Affordable Care Act's 2.5% in federal taxes are also added to every premium dollar.

When considering the high volume and reoccurrence of office visit and prescriptions, this 15% to 20% cost of convenience adds up to thousands of dollars in wasteful expenditures. And it is all hidden in premiums and payroll deductions.

Plans that allow for HSAs require the patient to pay the specialist $150 in this example, counting the entire claim towards deductible satisfaction. This eliminates the $20 - $25 tax and processing charge, reducing premium costs and payroll contributions.

Specialist Office Visit Example

$150 Specialist Visit

$50 Copay & $100 Insurance Payment

$25 Administration & Taxes added to premium

$175 Total Cost

Or, Upfront Deductible Plan

$150 Payment with HRA or HSA

$0 Insurance Payment

$0 Administrative fee in premium

$150 Total Cost

FLEXIBLE SPENDING ACCOUNTS (FSA)

Flexible Spending Accounts (FSA), a Section 125 benefit, allows the pre-tax payment of qualified health expenses as outlined in Section 213d of the Internal Revenue Code. For many years FSAs enjoyed limited interest because of the "use it or lose it rule", included by lawmakers so that participants accepted risk to pay for health care costs pre-tax.

Significant growth in FSA participation has occurred since 2005 due to increasing copay and deductible responsibility and the two and a half month reimbursement extension. The ability to pay pre-tax for many "Over the Counter" products and therapies also increased FSA awareness and participation. The Affordable Care Act stripped FSAs of this feature unless physicians write a prescription for Over the Counter products.

Debit card technology that allows ease of payment for FSA purchases, and the "uniform coverage" rule requiring employers to fund annual deferral amounts "at time of need" prior to full collection of FSA deferrals adds to the appeal of these accounts. A tax-free, interest-free "loan" is afforded participants that spend their annual FSA deferral early in the year.

FSAs now also allow for the upfront payment of scheduled services such as orthodontia treatment. In addition, Debit cards may be loaded with after tax funds to assist employees with additional out of pocket cash flow needs.

The IRS requires substantiation documentation that FSA funds have been used only for qualified Section 213d expenses. Follow up substantiation paperwork must be sent to the FSA administrator, generally within 30 days of a debit card purchase. If not provided, the debit card will stop working unless the participant agrees to reimburse unauthorized usage or have an after tax payroll deduction to reimburse their employer.

Auto-Substantiation can fortunately occur at times thanks to electronic approval standards. The Inventory Information Approval System (IIAS) allows for electronic approvals including copayments and reoccurring qualified expenses at the same cost.

DRIP VERSUS GUSHER PROTECTION

Income "drips" from every paycheck to fund an FSA, while 100% of the annual amount promised is available at time of need. A leap of faith is necessary to appreciate FSA Section 125 plan tax savings. The tax benefit shows up in one's paycheck, because the Section 125 deduction is "above the line". So a $100 per pay deferral reduces one's paycheck by $70 on average. Unfortunately for some FSAs do not "sizzle." Paychecks include so many deductions today that voluntarily adding another reduction to take home pay is not attractive, even if pre-tax.

Repeat FSA users are drawn to participate again and again once "gusher" payments are received for the annual amount set aside. When $1,500 or more is needed to satisfy a health insurance deductible, and all of the funds are "on the card", cash flow is protected. Having one's paycheck reduced $30 every week, with net take home pay adjusted down $20, resulting in access to $1,500 when needed, exemplifies how the FSA acts as a wonderful cash flow tool.

At plan year-end, unused FSA amounts are considered "experience gains" for the employer and may be used to offset administrative expenses, or returned to employees in a reasonable and uniform basis. Unsubstantiated FSA expenses may generate a future year W-2 taxable responsibility. The Affordable Care Act limits FSA deferrals to a maximum of $2,500 per worker.

Sub Chapter S Corporation owners, directors and partners are not allowed to participate in FSAs. Discrimination rules requiring annual tests to confirm that highly compensated employees do not defer more than lower paid employees is a responsibility in managing FSAs.

Pre-tax deferrals for parking or transit costs and dependent care may be offered as part of an FSA. These deferral options are often included alongside medical care FSA plans. Maximum annual pre-tax deferrals for parking and transit approach $3,000. Dependent care deferrals up to $5,000 are allowed for joint tax return filers. Access to these funds is limited to deposits made, or "money in, money out". Vendors must provide their business Tax ID number in order for parents to take advantage of these non-health care FSAs.

Limited and post-deductible FSAs may be offered in tandem with Health Savings Accounts (HSAs). Limited FSAs allow pre-tax dental and vision payments prior to satisfaction of the HSA deductible. A limited FSA also allows pre-tax payment of qualified medical services once the HSA deductible has been satisfied. Limited FSAs are of value to parents of children with orthodontia expenses. HSA owners who do not want expensive non-medical costs to deplete their HSA are attracted to limited FSAs.

HSAs & FSAs Tax Savings Example

- FIT (Federal)   18%
- FICA   7.65%
- State   3.35%
- <u>Local   1%</u>
- Total   30%

<u>$30 saved in taxes for every $100 spent pre-tax</u>

HEALTH REIMBURSEMENT ARRANGEMENTS

A popular option to navigate cost efficiency is available with Health Reimbursement Arrangements (HRA). These are employer offered plans that reimburse participants for a portion of out of pocket costs. HRAs have been available since 2002 and are often referred to as Health Reimbursement Accounts.

Employers who introduce upfront deductible plans often implement HRAs to reimburse a portion of insurance plan deductibles.

One must think retrospectively to embrace the rationale for HRAs. A $100 deductible 30 years ago has about the same value as a $1,000 deductible today. Employers that implement higher deductible plans use an HRA to "back-fill" a portion of employee out-of-pocket exposure.

HRAs help reduce health care expenses in that:

1. Lower claims costs result from plans with upfront deductibles. This translates to reduced premiums.
2. Awareness of the value and cost of health care products and services increases for participants with HRAs.
3. Because 40% to 60% of the promised HRA benefit is used, employers offer a more generous first dollar benefit to employees than with HMO,

48

POS, PPO copay plans and amounts deposited into HSAs.

An HRA must be offered on a nondiscriminatory basis. Plan designs are generally limited to covering a portion of in-network services subject to deductible satisfaction. This is a significant difference versus funding HSAs, which do not include limitations, other than penalties and taxation, on how the individual may spend reimbursement funds. (*Unlike a typical HRA, HSA and FSA funds may be used to pay for out of network health care services.*)

The option exists to allow unused HRA funds to rollover to the next year, and at times this makes sense, minimizing the need to increase the HRA amount if deductibles increase in future years.

As with FSAs, Sub Chapter S Corporation owners, directors and partners are not allowed to participate in an HRA.

HRA plans are most appreciated when reimbursing the first half of an upfront deductible, maximizing positive plan perception as on average 75% of participants end up with $0 net out of pocket health care costs. Creative designs also reimburse a portion of the deductible up front, followed by a personal responsibility portion and then more in HRA reimbursements if claims costs are high enough. At times the second half of a deductible is reimbursed.

HRAs can also reimburse certain copays along with a portion of coinsurance responsibility.

Back filling "out of pocket" cost exposure maintains affordability and is efficiently achieved when HRAs are coupled with FSAs. One Debit card may be offered to access both **HRA & FSA** funds. When you know you will spend the entire deductible in health care expenses, having 100% of funds available on the Debit Card eliminates cash flow concerns.

Health Reimbursement Account (HRA)

- 1st Dollar reimbursement of in-network deductible expenses
- Debit Card provided
- 1st $1,250 individual
- 1st $2,500 with dependents
- No Rollover of unused funds
- 60% loss ratio

When rolling out an HDHP, offering an HRA instead of HSAs is a common strategy as:

A. A projected 60% loss ratio allows employers to promise more money to offset deductible expenses than with HSAs.

B. 100% of the promised HRA amount is available at time of need vs. HSAs where only on deposit amounts may be withdrawn.

C. Expected "out of pocket" costs above the HRA may be deferred using a pre-tax FSA.

HRAs are self-insured plans designed to reduce out of pocket risk while training employees and their dependents to increase awareness of the true cost of health care services.

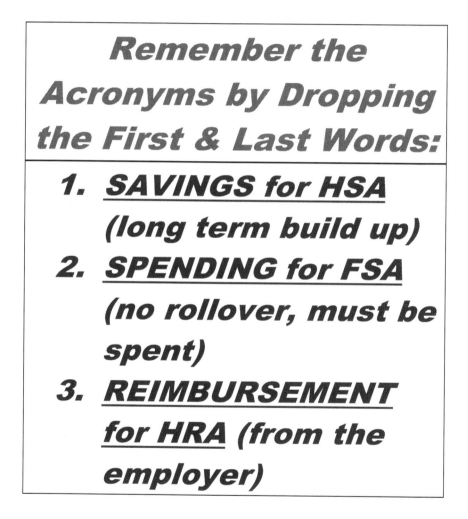

Remember the Acronyms by Dropping the First & Last Words:

1. <u>*SAVINGS* for *HSA*</u> (long term build up)
2. <u>*SPENDING* for *FSA*</u> (no rollover, must be spent)
3. <u>*REIMBURSEMENT* for *HRA*</u> (from the employer)

VI. Protecting Cash Flow with Debit Cards

MasterCard® technology enhances cash flow and pre-tax spending power. A smart card allowing for payment of out of pocket health care expenses has been available for many years, easing cash flow as we navigate paying increasing personal out of pocket expenses.

With HSAs, as long as there are funds in the account, a debit card can be used to pay for health care expenses. With an HRA, 100% of the promised amount can be accessed at time of need with one's debit card. And thanks to the Uniform Coverage rules for FSAs, 100% of the annual deferral can be accessed at time of need anytime during the plan year. The exposure of deductibles and other out of pocket risk is thus neutralized thanks to instant, electronic access to funds.

Choosing an Upfront Deductible health plan requires investing in the financial management of one's health care expenses. Accepting personal responsibility that providers of care get paid in full is necessary until the deductible is satisfied. As long as in-network doctors and hospitals are used, negotiated, discounted prices are accepted as payment in full.

The purchase of prescriptions is straight- forward. When visiting a pharmacy or mailing away for prescriptions, providing health insurance coverage confirmation along with a limited use MasterCard® debit card. Prescriptions are instantly discounted at the time of purchase, finalized by swiping the card.

Limited use, health-care-only debit cards are "PIN-less" No Personal Identification Number (PIN) is required. The card is also "category code restricted" and will not work to purchase gasoline or at a restaurant. This is what makes it "smart".

Purchasing a prescription is straightforward while hospital and doctor visit payments add time to the cycle. At the time of a visit, the office staff checks your insurance card or an online system to confirm coverage. Payment is due after the claim is processed by the insurance company, not at the completion of the visit.

The office staff bills the insurance company, listing their "charge". The insurer discounts the charge and mails, or provides electronically an EOB (Explanation of Benefits) to the billing office and the patient's home. The EOB lists the charge and the discounted, covered amount that is due.

An invoice is mailed by the health care provider to the patient, who is responsible for paying the provider the discounted amount. The patient has the option to fill in the numbers from their debit card on the invoice and mail it back, allowing electronic payment from the MasterCard ®.

If the office staff demands a copayment, and the card is active, agree to a $20 swipe from your debit card and be certain this shows up as a credit when they send their invoice.

If the provider does not accept debit card payments, the patient must pay directly with cash or check and request reimbursement from their HRA/FSA/HSA administrator.

The administrator generally demands substantiation of a debit card payment for HRA and FSA usage. By taking a picture of an EOB with a smart phone using a mobile app, or scanning and emailing documentation, or faxing of an EOB, validation occurs. The IRS maintains standards for ensuring a health care purchase is a qualified, tax-deductible expense. Employers are also required to audit use of HRA funds to confirm payments are only for covered services.

Funds available on the debit card may be exhausted before one's out-of-pocket responsibility is satisfied. In this situation, there is personal payment responsibility. Deferring enough money into an FSA eliminates the inconvenience of deductible exposure, and reduces taxes.

Health care debit card systems ultimately know whether a service is HRA and/or FSA eligible.

Banks and administrators will continue to develop payment systems to enhance HRA/FSA documentation efficiency. Debit card technology is also being developed to allow for less than 100% payment of a covered service to reduce employer HRA costs. Someday winners at the health care game will be able to swipe a smart card and the provider will be paid the discounted amount without having the extra step of substantiation.

Potentially straightforward and simple, but there are times the Debit Card breaks down:

1. What if the office staff demands a copayment upfront?
2. What if the provider office does not accept debit card payments?
3. What if the administrator requires "substantiation" back up to confirm the debit card was used for proper purchases?
4. What if there are no funds available on the debit card?
5. What if the card has been "shut off" because prior usage has not been properly substantiated?

VII. Bio-Metric, Metabolic, Preventive Care & Wellness Incentive Programs

It really does make a difference and is critical to win the health care game. Exercise and moderate consumption enhances quality of life and saves money on health care. A few French fries, candy and cookies keep life from being bland, and totally eliminating cake and ice cream is not required. Recognition and awareness of moderation and exercise techniques is a growing business because people know they need to change habits that have evolved from their upbringing.

The numbers to beat are not unreasonable for most of us.

Bio-Metric, Metabolic Standards

1. **Cholesterol <200 mg/dl; LDL <130; HDL >40**
2. **Glucose <100 mg/dl**
3. **Blood Pressure <140 systolic <90 diastolic**
4. **Body Mass Index <30 kg./m2**
5. **Carbon Monoxide <5 parts per million**

After a four hour fast, a small amount of blood is drawn by a technician who is able in 20 minutes to report cholesterol and glucose levels. While the analysis is in progress, other tests are administered along with a confidential discussion about health history and lifestyle habits. If any of the numbers are beyond an acceptable range, counseling is provided with the goal of promoting change.

Another test opportunity may occur six to twelve months in the future to gauge progress. The incentive may be rewarded for maintaining three or more of these standards. Or, an incentive is awarded per standard maintained. The point is that all of these levels are controllable through diet, avoidance, exercise and at times diligently taking one's prescribed medicines.

PPACA also allows up to a 50% incentive for programs designed to reduce and prevent undesirable effects from smoking. Formal testing and honor code systems are used for monitoring, including Commitment Contracts where funds are set aside daily equal to a specified amount, possibly the cost of a pack of cigarettes, with an award six months later assuming nicotine or carbon monoxide fall within norms. Online Health Assessments, sometimes referred to as Health Risk Assessments, coupled with support steps to correct early onset medical conditions, work to maximize one's quality of life once an ongoing action plan for good health commences.

When employers invest in health & wellness programs it positively impacts the bottom line by increasing work attendance and quality of output. The addition of Online Medical Records data is being promoted to consolidate the monitoring of personal health factors with education of patients on ways to improve health. The bottom line goal is for these evolving tools to reduce health care costs.

To keep cars and trucks running, periodic maintenance is a necessity. The same concept applies to personal health. Try visiting the onsite clinic at work and take advantage of preventive exams covered by your health plan. Or schedule a preventive physical exam with your doctor, paid at 100%. Mammograms at age 40 and colonoscopies at age 50 are proven lifesavers, and are 100% covered in PPACA health insurance plans.

Re-occurring face to face wellness coaching at the worksite yields a strong return on investment. This system of engagement becomes personal and assists not only the employee. It is likely to spill over positively affecting spouse and children's health habits.

Promoting a combination of daily physical activity, moderation in food and alcohol consumption, the elimination of tobacco consumption and periodic health checkups reduces "risk factors" and their expense. Good habits can be even further supported with stress reduction through Spirituality with a sense of faith and hope. Peace of mind is good for productivity and our sense of purpose.

Incentives by some are considered disincentives to others. If an employer increases payroll

contributions for health insurance and then waives the increase for the healthier participants, or offers extra deposits to Health Savings Accounts, Flexible Spending Accounts or a Health Reimbursement Arrangement for those with successful test results, this may be perceived as a stick and not a carrot. Expect these strategies to become more common and fundamental to winning the health care game.

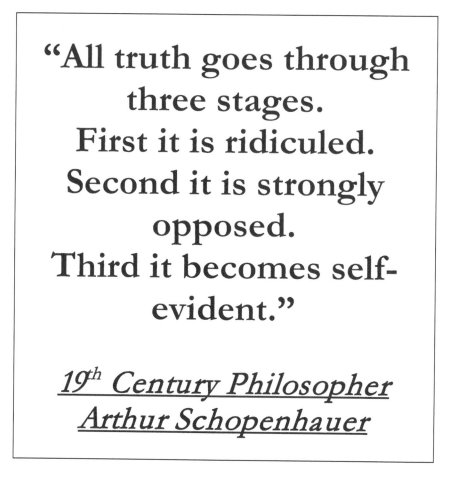

"All truth goes through three stages.
First it is ridiculed.
Second it is strongly opposed.
Third it becomes self-evident."

19th Century Philosopher
Arthur Schopenhauer

VIII. Value Based Plans - Caring For Yourself as a Health Care Consumer

As we navigate the new health insurance marketplace, recent trends to reduce catastrophic health insurance costs include proactively monitoring selected patients that are chronically ill. "Value Based Plans" are built on patient compliance with doctor visit schedules, testing, diet and taking prescribed medicines. "Out of pocket" cost waivers are offered as an incentive to hopefully reduce future catastrophic care needs for patients who are already ill. Think of the diabetic, severe asthmatic or post heart attack patient that does not have the funds to budget for reoccurring out of pocket medical expenses. They are chosen for monitoring in Value Based Plans.

Patients qualify for these waivers once confirmed by their health care history. They must "sign up" and agree to see a select group of providers on a re-occurring basis, along with promising to take their medicine each day. In addition they agree to a personalized diet and exercise regimen. Medical Homes in the PPACA law align with this approach.

These patients become health care consumers by committing to using health care resources in the most efficient setting for monitoring their illnesses.

Personal cost neutralization may be managed through the health insurance plan design or in a more simplified way by using a specialized Health Reimbursement

Arrangement (HRA) to cover deductible, copay and coinsurance out of pocket expenses.

Value Based Plans financially favor the sick in the eyes of some, but this argument does not hold up once all factors are considered:

1. Ill patients who have their out of pocket costs reimbursed lose various freedoms including health care at their provider of choice.
2. Savings in claims costs when catastrophic care expenses are avoided reduces costs for the entire covered population.

Value Based Plans may also be designed to reduce deductible exposure for those who agree to complete periodic Health Risk Evaluations, along with having Biometrics tested. This type of consumerism can catch health care problems early, such as untreated high blood pressure, a "silent killer" because it lacks clear symptoms.

Differing levels of awards and incentives may be built into Value Based Plans so that participants whose Biometric results fall within acceptable levels receive rewards such as additional HRA or HSA credits. Winning the health care game requires being open-minded about helping the sick and needy for the greater good.

IX. Medicare – When I'm 65 or maybe 70

American seniors are winners at the health care game having access to retiree health insurance coverage that became law 50 years ago. Navigating these health insurance options can be overwhelming when reaching the Medicare eligibility age. The terminology is vexing. There are "Parts" in addition to "Plans". Some of the insurance is already paid for and some require making payments until Social Security kicks in and then it is deducted from that retirement check. It quickly comes to light that Medicare alone is not good enough insurance resulting in the need to purchase wrap around coverage or Medicare Advantage.

Seniors purchasing a MediGap plan (wraparound / supplement), plus prescription Rx coverage, end up with four types of coverage. Three of the four require premium payments. The option of purchasing one Medicare Advantage plan results in one or two premium payments, and yet if you travel extensively or have a second home in a different state, you will be ill advised to enroll in a Medicare Advantage plan due to the lack of in network hospitals and doctors where you travel.

It may seem complicated, but like learning to press ten telephone numbers on the telephone versus seven, we all grow into change over time.

Medicare started in 1965 when President Harry Truman and his wife Bess first enrolled. It now insures 40+

million retirees and disabled Americans. Retirees must reach age 65 to be eligible. Medicare Part A, which covers hospitalization needs, requires no premium for enrollees who have worked and made payroll tax payments for less than 40 quarters (ten years). Credit towards Part A is automatically provided to spouses. They may not have worked outside of the home, but are credited for their contribution as the "Family Manager". Enrollees who have worked fewer than 10 years are required to pay up to $5,000 per year in premium for this protection.

Payroll taxes equal to 1.45% of income provide funding for Medicare Part A. With The Affordable Care Act, 2.35% of income earned in excess of $200,000 is taxed if filing individually. The increase to 2.35% begins at $250,000 if filing a joint tax return.

Unknown too many younger workers is that Medicare Part B, which covers the cost of physician services, is a voluntary program. Monthly premiums for this coverage are typically deducted from Social Security benefit checks. There are four premium levels based upon income, ranging from $100 to more than $300 per person per month. Retiring couples must double these amounts to properly calculate their total monthly premium responsibility.

If one continues to work fulltime at age 65 for a business with fewer than 20 employees, Medicare Parts A & B act as primary insurance for hospitalization and physician services. If one works full-time for a larger employer, the employer's plan is primary, meaning it pays first. It may not be financially advantageous to sign up for Social Security and Medicare until retirement if in this type of circumstance.

There is no penalty for delaying Medicare enrollment to a later time if working for a larger employer as long as you maintain active worker coverage. Although dis-enrolling from the employer's plan is allowed, employers may not induce Medicare eligible workers to move to Medicare for primary insurance. It has rarely, if ever been financially beneficial for the Medicare eligible worker to dis-enroll from their employer's plan and move voluntarily to Medicare.

<u>MEDICARE IS NOT RICH INSURANCE</u>

Medicare Part A & B benefit levels are inferior to private health insurance. In 2008, the Medicare Part A deductible exceeded $1,000 for the first time, which equated to a 32% increase over the Calendar Year 2000 deductible of $776. The deductible rises almost every year climbing to $1,184 in 2013, 56% higher than in CY 2000.

Long term hospitalization under Part A is not covered at 100%, requiring significant payments per day. Costs after 60 days in patient can exceed $8,000, and there is even greater exposure from 90 to 150 days, when out of pocket costs can exceed $35,000. This government coverage can even be exhausted.

The Affordable Care Act requires unlimited lifetime coverage for Americans under age 65 and limits out of pocket cost exposure to just over $6,000 single and $12,000 family per year. Similar limits do not exist with Medicare.

Medicare Part B includes a nominal deductible of around $150, but then requires 20% coinsurance forever; never transitioning to 100% coverage for physician services and diagnostic tests. A $10,000 physician expense results in $2,000+ in personal cost responsibility. These two realities are why most seniors purchase additional coverage.

Once retired, many seniors purchase a MediGap (wraparound / supplement) plan to pay some or all of what Medicare Part A & B does not pick up, such as deductibles and coinsurance. These "Plans" use a lettering system and are named Plans A though N. They are all offered by private insurers. Plans C & F are most popular because all deductible and coinsurance costs are paid in full. They also cost the most in premium.

In 2006, prescription Rx plans under Medicare Part D became available for purchase. Part D Rx plans are all sold by private insurers, who must offer policies that provide Creditable Coverage. Insurers generally offer two or three plan options. The least expensive Part D Rx plan provides the minimum Creditable, or legal coverage amount. There are $300 plus deductibles to meet plus 25% coinsurance to pay under the lowest premium Part D Rx plans. More expensive Part D Rx plans include copays per prescription purchased and may provide generic medicine coverage through the "Rx hole in the doughnut".

The "Rx Hole in the Doughnut" concept is a brilliant solution to a challenging insurance coverage conundrum. The Affordable Care Act eliminates the doughnut hole by 2020, replacing it with 25% coinsurance. Medicare Part D has cost the government less to subsidize than originally forecasted in part because of the doughnut hole. Part D has been a financial success, although the doughnut hole "gap" is too significant, making expensive drugs unaffordable for some seniors.

Medicare Advantage plans are offered by private insurers as an alternative to Medicare A&B plus MediGap and are designed to include unlimited lifetime coverage protection. Most plans include copays for out of pocket costs. Some have high enough copays they do not require payment of a monthly premium, which serves well seniors with limited incomes. Some plans also include dental, vision and hearing aid coverage or discounts at select providers.

There are high deductible type Medicare Advantage plans available in selected markets. They are generally not popular as the savings in premium too often does not justify the risk assumed. Once the deductible in these plans is satisfied, covered health care expenses are paid at 100%, similar to upfront deductible plans for workers that allow a Health Savings Account.

INCREASED SAVINGS IF DELAYING RETIREMENT

Once enrolled in Social Security, Medicare Part A coverage starts. The option to deposit pre-tax funds into a Health Savings Account then ceases. If healthy and working until age 70 while covered under an upfront deductible plan that allows HSAs, this extends the time period for pre-tax HSA deposits, supplementing health care retirement savings. By delaying enrollment in Social Security to age 70, benefit payments increase by 8%. This is likely to be a consideration for more and more Americans desiring to win the health care game.

With age 60 being the new age 40, it may be that the Medicare eligibility age increases from age 65 to 70 if born in 1960 or later. This change is likely to occur in concert with new private insurer plan designs allowing Medicare coverage that is more flexible and comprehensive, and includes pre-tax health care savings opportunities.

MEDICARE FOR ALL

A "Medicare for All" system has been proposed by some as the answer to reining in American health care spending. If such an approach took hold, it would act as a breeding ground for private, supplemental health insurance, assuming basic Medicare coverage continues to be limited in the protections offered. It is an interesting concept to engage private insurers to offer "Medicare for All" supplemental coverage, with a government insurance acting as primary protection. This may be a winning strategy long term.

Passing laws in our great country involves compromise. A "Medicare for All", or Single Payor System may also lead to reduced access, rationing of care and a decrease in curative, technological investments. The hospitals and physicians end up totally on the government's payroll, beholden to the bureaucratic expectations of standardized treatment protocols. Let's be realistic. This may be the future anyway with PPACA.

Questions arise as to whether the greater good will be served in a "Medicare for All" system, as citizens in most other western countries already accept "one size fits all" government insurance.

Retired insurance buyers must pay premiums with after-tax dollars, unless they have built up reserves in a Health Savings Account to pay Medicare Advantage premiums. HSA pre-tax savings are not allowed to be used for payment of MediGap premiums. HSA pre-tax savings can also be used pre-tax for out of pocket costs and Long Term Care insurance premiums.

A little known fact is that private insurers act as government contractors processing all Medicare claims. The government takes the risk and insurance companies do the work.

Demographics & Changing Insurance Needs

Age 19– 39: Accidents, Allergies, Mostly Treatable Maladies & Maternity

Age 40 – 54: Some of the above plus Balding, Cancer, Obesity & Organ issues

Age 55 – 64: Some of the above plus Circulatory & Skeletal Breakdowns

Age 65+: Some of the above & End of Life Care

People Stories for Winning the Health Care Game
X. Employers & Employees who are Winning

How does this winning approach work in the real world? It is time to go beyond the hypothetical to actual examples slowing down and reversing health insurance cost increases. Since savings ultimately translates to payroll deductions for employees, the end result is increased take home pay enhancing quality of life and freeing up funds to save for future health care needs.

Employers adopting Upfront Deductible plan concepts improve their bottom line. Data confirms almost 10 years of flat or lower costs for certain employers during a period when double digit premium increases had been the norm. And savings success is not a function of size, location or type of population. Examples confirm that adopting upfront deductible plans is bullet proof and how best to win the health care game.

1. A manufacturing and distribution company covering 4,000 employees and family members introduced two Upfront Deductible plan options in 2004, replacing Point of Service (POS) copay plans. The employer reimbursed the first half of the deductible in one of the plans using an HRA. This plan included 10% coinsurance once the deductible was satisfied and cost more per pay than the alternative plan which included 20% coinsurance and no HRA.

The first year of this new offering 65% of the employees selected the more expensive plan with the HRA benefit, in part because it cost more per pay. Health care costs for the entire self-insured population remained flat for 4 consecutive years and more than half of the population remained in the plan with the HRA.

In 2008 the company scrapped the HRA and offered HSAs instead. This roll out included reducing payroll deductions by 50% coupled with depositing one-third of the upfront deductible as HSA contributions. Communications focused on promoting to employees the long term value of transferring their payroll deduction savings to supplement HSA deposits. Very smart!

2. A construction management company with 30 employees and family members introduced an upfront deductible health insurance plan in 2008 to avoid a premium rate increase.

All employees plus the owners transitioned to a $2,500 single and $5,000 family deductible PPO plan, followed by 100% coverage in network services except prescriptions, which were subject to copayments. The company reimbursed the first 75% of deductible expenses using an HRA and provided every covered adult a Debit Card.

That year 55% of the available HRA funds were spent resulting in an overall cost reduction of -16%. The company moved insurers in 2009, lowering costs by an additional 25%. Coinsurance of 10% capped at $1,000 was added post deductible in 2011.

Over a six year period, wages have risen more than the industry average and employee payroll deductions for health insurance have not changed. Health insurance costs are 41% lower than in 2007.

3. A manufacturing and distribution company with 225 employees and family members introduced an upfront deductible health insurance plan in 2008, avoiding a 16% rate jump. The group transitioned to a $2,500 single and $5,000 family deductible PPO plan, followed by 100% coverage for all in network services except prescriptions.

The company reimbursed the first 45% of deductible expenses using an HRA. An FSA was also introduced for employees to defer their own money pre-tax to efficiently pay for projected out of pocket health care expenses.

At the end of the first plan year, 51% of the available HRA funds were spent reimbursing deductible expenses. An overall 12% cost reduction occurred versus prior year expenses, which was equal to 28% in savings when compared to renewal rates that would have been paid if the prior plan had been continued.

In 2009 the company increased deductibles to $3,000 single and $6,000 family. The first dollar HRA was increased to 50% of the single deductible and 60% of the family deductible. Even with coverage improvement an additional 5% cost decrease resulted that year.

By 2012 an additional 16% cost reduction was negotiated to maintain the same plan and HRA. Over a six year period, employee payroll contributions for insurance coverage have been adjusted once, and health insurance costs are -11% lower than expenses in 2007.

4. An auto dealer with 350 employees and family members transitioned to upfront deductible plans in 2006. An HRA was offered that reimbursed the 1st quarter of the Deductible, followed by a gap, then reimbursing the 3rd quarter of the deductible. Hospital and surgical coverage transitioned to 100% after the deductible was satisfied. Copays were maintained for high volume, lower cost services including office visits and prescriptions.

Costs per employee seven years later were 3% lower than in 2005 and there have been only two nominal changes to payroll deductions.

5. In 2007 a competing automobile dealer with 200 employees and family members eliminated a 14% cost increase by transitioning from a copay plan for hospitalization to a $1,500 single and $3,000 family deductible plan, followed by 20% coinsurance capped at $2,000. The employer reimbursed the first half of the deductible through an HRA, along with half of the coinsurance, plus offered to roll over unused HRA funds.

Premium rates dropped two years in a row, resulting in multiple reductions to employee payroll deductions. After seven years with an upfront deductible plan that includes copayments for office visits and prescriptions, the average annual premium increase per year has equaled 1.7%.

6. A multi-dimensional warehousing and distribution business eliminated a 27% premium increase in 2004 by moving their employees to a $1,000 single and $2,000 family deductible plan, followed by 10% coinsurance to $1,000. The company reimbursed the first half of the deductible using an HRA and maintained copays for office visits and Rx. Premium expenses were reduced an additional 8% the following year after changing to a qualified high deductible health plan.

Employees experienced no increase to payroll deductions over a four year time period. After nine years with an upfront deductible plan, health plan costs are 4% below levels in 2004, and FSAs are used by 65% of the workforce.

6. In order to avoid an 18% premium increase to their HMO plan, an urban health center with more 150 employees and family members moved to a $3,000 single and $6,000 family deductible, then 100% HDHP coverage plan. Premium savings were so substantial management chose to reimburse 90% of the deductible using an HRA.

At the end of the year, 78% of the available HRA funds were spent, translating to a 9% savings compared with the HMO plan, and a 27% cost reduction versus renewing the HMO plan. And virtually all employees had 100% of their health care expenses paid in full.

The HRA was too generous, adding to future rate increases of +16% followed by +18% and +22%. Time was proving that a plan where employees had almost zero responsibility for out of pocket expenses lacked a sense of consumerism.

At the outset of the fourth plan year, HSAs were offered as an option and the HRA amount available was reduced to 70% of the deductible. This turned the corner as costs were 3% lower than the prior year, with 35% of the group opting for HSAs.

There are many, many more examples of employers and employees transitioning to the upfront deductible approach, confirming its long term success flattening or reducing health plan costs. Take home pay increases over time with these types of health plan approaches that increase cost awareness and include opportunities to neutralize risk exposure.

The future is clear that employers will offer and workers will increasingly accept deductible and coinsurance based plan designs in order to pay lower premiums. Offering more expensive copay plans as options in defined contribution private exchange programs is already a consequence of "The Affordable Care Act". Workers resistant to change who prefer the simplicity of copay plans will begrudgingly pay more for convenience. Overall this combination of choices may be the best prescription for bending down the health care cost curve.

XI. *Single Ann's Wisdom Counselor*

For Ann, she felt like a winner and looked at it as her best investment of the year. Her co-workers made out just as well navigating through the company's new health insurance options.

Growing up, Ann's mother Helen worked two days a week in an insurance office. She was always in a great mood and made the tastiest meals after a day resolving claims issues for people. Ann did not know what it was about insurance that intrigued her, yet Mom always said, **"You should pay for good insurance, because you never know when you will need it."**

Ann, like most of us, had assumed the more expensive the health insurance plan the better. She first questioned this premise when her employer began promoting:

A. Plan options with low payroll contributions and upfront deductibles
B. HRA & FSA pre-tax accounts to cover qualified health care expenses not paid by insurance
C. HSAs for long term savings
D. 100% catastrophic protection versus never ending copays

When Ann went online to view the Open Enrollment information, she was intrigued by the Deductible plan being offered by her employer. Payroll deductions seemed too low. This did interest her because she and her fiancé were trying to save money for a down payment on a new home.

She then looked at the coverage details and was at first deflated. <u>Before the plan paid anything, she had to satisfy a $2,500 deductible!</u> The deductible applied to hospital stays, surgery, lab work, x-rays, office visits and even prescriptions. The only services covered in full were for preventive care visits.

Her perception improved as she read that her employer was offering to reimburse the FIRST HALF, or $1,250 of the deductible. It sounded interesting, but she was not certain the risk was worth it. Plus, she had been raised to believe you always pay for good insurance, because you never know when you may need it.

Ann brought up the new high deductible option during a visit with her mother at Helen's long term care facility. Ann's mother had retired a few years back, progressively losing the use of her legs.

Helen's mind though was as sharp as ever. She read two newspapers a day, spent time online with her tablet computer, plus enjoyed a weekly business magazine. Helen was known to reference in conversation all kinds of articles about insurance, including the health care reform.

After Ann described the new plan option, Helen posed these questions:

A. How much will you save next year in payroll deductions with the high deductible plan?
B. Can you estimate how much you will likely spend in copays?
C. Does your company offer a Flexible Spending Account?
E. Is the $1,000 paid by your employer available through a Health Reimbursement Arrangement (HRA) or a Health Savings Account (HSA)?
F. Is the level of coverage 100% after the deductible has been satisfied, or are you responsible for 10% to 20% of ongoing bills?

Ann initially struggled to grasp the significance of these points as the concepts were new to her. She also knew her mother would be disappointed if she did not have the details by the time of her next visit. She discovered a Q&A section developed by her employer and ultimately confirmed the answers before visiting Helen, which included an email to her employer's human resources group to confirm the answers to Helen's questions.

First Ann compared her current plan's cost of $100 per pay to the upfront deductible plan at $50 per pay. Her pay would increase $1,300 per year if she chose the high deductible plan. Next she looked at copays this year for medical care, and figured out that four office visits cost $150 out of pocket, an x-ray of her wrist after slipping on the ice cost $150 out of pocket, and her prescriptions cost $300 per year. Ann budgeted $600 out-of-pocket in copays.

Since her employer was now offering a voluntary Flexible Spending Account (FSA) program that allows pre-tax payment of out-of-pocket health expenses, she would have saved 30% in taxes equivalent to $160 in the year now ending, if out of pocket copays had been funneled through an FSA. Ann also learned that the $1,250 from her employer was available either through a HRA or an HSA, and not taxable compensation.

Her mother had questioned the how much the plan covered after the high deductible. Ann printed the plan summaries to compare both options and felt good about being prepared to discuss the answers.

During their next visit, Helen's first question kind of surprised her, and made her chuckle. Her Mom asked whether Ann had already decided on the new plan. "Why would I do that before seeking your advice, Mom" she said. "Because you usually already have your mind made up by the time you come to me."

"Well, I like the fact that I can reduce payroll deductions and increase my take home pay and the maximum out of pocket cap of $5,000 is the same in both plans. I save on copays since the first half of the deductible is 100% reimbursed. It looks like I might save close to $2,000 if I change. But what am I missing? Isn't it too good to be true?"

Helen asked to see the plan summaries and clarified that in the new plan, once the deductible has been satisfied in-network, the coverage is 90% for hospitalization, lab tests, emergency and doctor's office visits up to a total $5,000 out of pocket maximum. Prescriptions are subject to copays after the deductible is satisfied.

"Do you understand that 10% coinsurance post deductible satisfaction leaves you with another $2,500 in out of pocket risk? So although you get the first $1,250 upfront, worst case you could spend $3,750 if you have a major problem."

"Of course, under the copay plan, five nights in the hospital requires you to spend $2,000 in copays, and the total out of pocket maximum is $4,000." This was Helen's way of making certain that Ann really grasped coinsurance, which had been common in health insurance plans before the 1990s.

"The new plan has appeal the more that I study the details, especially since the odds are low that you will need high cost care. And the $1,250 upfront will more than pay for the care you normally need. **Your current copay plan 'nickels and dimes' you every time you receive or purchase health care services. The new plan does not.**

Qualified High Deductible Plan	In NETWORK	Out of NETWORK
	HRA or HSAs	
Benefits and Services	**$1,250 SINGLE / $2,500 FAMILY**	
Annual Deductible		
Individual	$2,500	$5,000
Family	$5,000	$10,000
After Deductible Plan Pays	90%	50%
Out of Pocket Limit		
Individual	$5,000	$10,000
Family	$10,000	$20,000
Lifetime Maximum	Unlimited	Unlimited
Preventive Care	100%, no Deductible	50%
Women's Health	100%, no Deductible	50%
Routine Physical	100%, no Deductible	50%
Routine GYN Exam	100%, no Deductible	50%
Well Child Care	100%, no Deductible	50%
Emergency Room	After Deductible, 90%	50%
Physician Office	After Deductible, 90%	50%
Specialist Office	After Deductible, 90%	50%
Chiropractic	After Deductible, 90%	50%
Inpatient Hospital	After Deductible, 90%	50%
Outpatient Hospital	After Deductible, 90%	50%
Maternity	After Deductible, 90%	50%
Surgery and Anesthesia	After Deductible, 90%	50%
Lab / X-Ray	After Deductible, 90%	50%
Physical Therapy	After Deductible, 90%	50%
Inpatient Psychiatric	After Deductible, 90%	50%
Outpatient Psychiatric	After Deductible, 90%	50%
Prescription Drugs	***After Deductible is Satisfied***	
Retail Rx	$10 Generic / $40 Preferred / $60 NP	
Mail Order Rx	$30 Generic / $80 Preferred / $120 NP	

Ann confirmed to Helen that she could receive the entire HRA $1,250 immediately as needed. The FSA allowed her to reduce her pay to cover the second $1,250 of the deductible on a pre-tax basis, if she chose to set money aside.

She would be cautious with FSA deferral amount because of the "Use it Or Lose It" rule, and yet appreciated knowing the option existed. Helen's insurance knowledge kicked in as she scribbled the following comparison.

Current Plan:	$2,600 in payroll deductions
	$ 600 in expected copays
	$3,200 KNOWN COST
Additional risk:	$4,400 to out of pocket cap
Max Exposure	**$7,600**
New Plan:	$1,300 in payroll deductions
	$0 in deductible
	$1,300 KNOWN COST
Additional risk:	$3,750 to out of pocket cap
Total	**$5,050**
Expected Savings:	*$1,900*
Worst Case Savings:	*$2,250*

"I'm surprised they call it a High Deductible Health Plan, since when you compound inflation, the purchasing power of $1,250 is equal to $125 just twenty-five years ago. Do you think you have made up your mind now?" Helen asked.

"I have decided on the Upfront Deductible plan with the HRA. Worst case I am better off and in a normal year way ahead. The entire $1,250 is available when needed using the HRA and the same is true for what I may deposit into the FSA.

Even though 50% of the HSA funds will be deposited at the beginning of the year with the balance each pay, saving money to buy a house is more important now than saving for my future health care costs. Someday I will want an HSA, but now protecting my cash flow and saving to buy a house are more important."

Helen felt a sense of thanks that her daughter made a winning decision. She decided to add to her final wishes that a portion of the money left to Ann be spent on necessities, freeing up income for her to start a pre-tax HSA for long term savings.

XII. *Dave & Doris' Best Choice*

Ann's boss Dave was very interested in the process she and Helen had gone through concluding that the Upfront Deductible plan as the better choice. His family included spouse Doris and three teenage age children. Dave and Doris had recently celebrated 25 years of marriage.

She was in charge of dealing with the family's medical care needs. They rarely discussed health insurance at home, except for the hassles that came up obtaining prescription approvals to treat the asthma of their youngest child. The copay for one medicine was $60 per month, which seemed like a lot of money until they found out that the medicine's real cost was $150.

Their current plan for the family was increasing in cost to $200 per pay, or $5,200 per year. Deductions for the Upfront Deductible plan were $120 per pay, or $3,120 per year, a savings of $2,080. The deductible was $5,000 for the family, with the first $2,500 given to them by the company through an HRA or an HSA.

Dave knew the asthma medicine alone cost $1,800 for the year, versus current copays of $700. Doris and he sat at the kitchen table after dinner one night and figured out their entire copay costs. The family used 6 maintenance medicines each month and averaged 12 office visit appointments. Since some of these were to treat sinus infections, the necessary antibiotics resulted in 3 additional prescriptions. They anticipated at least one emergency room visit per year including an x-ray, so projected a total of $1,800 in copays.

Current Plan: $5,200 in payroll deductions
                   $1,800 in expected copays
                   $7,000 KNOWN COST
Additional risk: $8,200 to out of pocket cap
Max Exposure: $15,200

New Plan: $3,000 in payroll deductions
                   $2,500 in deductible
                   $5,500 KNOWN COST
Additional risk: $5,000 to out of pocket cap
Max Exposure: $13,000

Expected Savings: *$1,500*
Worst Case Savings: *$2,200*

The family knew they could easily spend the entire $5,000 deductible during a normal year, and have more out of pocket costs for prescription copays and coinsurance. But they still saved money with the Upfront Deductible plan by deferring an additional $3,500 in an HSA so their deductible and coinsurance costs could all be paid with pre-tax dollars, saving at least $1,000 in income taxes.

If they had a year in health care costs that did not include any accidents or major illnesses, a portion of their HSA deferral would roll over to the next plan year and build pre-tax interest earnings. And fortunately they had an IRA they could tap into to transfer funds into the HSA if health care expenses were higher than expected.

A winning team with 25 years of marriage to show for it included having the best of both rubbing off on each other. Doris who was frugal by nature had helped Dave to see the light on budgeting to enhance marital bliss. Dave knew how to keep it all fun with a knack for romance. Amazing the impact of making certain they kept up their date nights together as a couple.

XIII. _Amy & Joe's Mature Analysis_

Dave told his co-worker Amy who assisted the big boss that he was moving to the new plan. **At first incredulous, she asked "You do well financially, why not buy the best?"** He replied that saving for college tuition was a financial hurdle, so the family was always open to new ideas that could free up cash. "By the way, that Upfront Deductible option may be best for your husband and you", he exclaimed.

Amy had recovered from breast cancer three years prior and appreciated their lack of insurance hassles other than always paying copays. Now age 60, their macrobiotic cooking regimen had helped Joe and her to lose weight, plus eliminated the need for cholesterol and blood pressure medicine. He was also 60 and had his own construction and landscaping business. He loved the outdoors. Their children were grown and out on their own. It was exciting their third grandchild was due in a month.

Amy decided to heed Dave's advice and study the Upfront Deductible plan option. She learned that the upfront deductible for Joe and her would be $5,000. Her payroll deductions dropped from $180 per pay to $100 per pay, a savings of $2,080 per year. Dave had given her the worksheet from Ann's mother.

Current Plan:	$4,680 in payroll deductions
	$ 320 in expected copays
	$5,000 KNOWN COST
Additional risk:	$9,680
Max Exposure:	**$14,680**
New Plan:	$2,600 in payroll deductions
	$0 in deductible
	$2,600 KNOWN COST
Additional risk:	$7,500 to out of pocket cap
Max Exposure:	**$12,600**
Expected Savings:	*$2,400*
Worst Case Savings:	*$2,080*

The interesting part about the HSA idea included the ability to deposit almost $5,000 tax-free above the $2,500 provided by the employer into their own HSA bank account. They were old enough to qualify for the "catch-up" rule, allowing an additional $1,000 per year to be deferred from age 55 until Medicare eligibility. Because unused HSA funds rollover, it offered them an opportunity to generate additional tax-free savings. Assuming they remained healthy, by the time they retired, $40,000 or more in health care retirement savings would be available in addition to their 401k plan savings. A winner!

Joe liked that this new plan meant they no longer had to hassle with never ending copayments. He understood the payment risk upfront the first year because the HSA money accumulated per pay. Fortunately they had a "rainy day" reserve in their savings account, so if a costly health care bill occurred prior to building an HSA reserve, money was available to deposit into the HSA to pay the balance of the $5,000 deductible. At the same time, building this type of Emergency Fund offered additional peace of mind.

Amy and Joe knew hospitalization is expensive. Chronic care needs can be very costly when you must return again and again for treatment, paying a copayment each visit, as she experienced after her breast cancer. They supported parts of the new health care reform law, since for the health care system to work efficiently patients should not have the risk of outrageous out of pocket costs for their care needs at the same time people become aware of the true cost of quality health care.

XIV. _Robyn's Winning Leadership Rationale_

Amy told the big boss Robyn about why she was moving to the Upfront Deductible plan. When she explained that it all started with Ann and her mother Helen, you could see a winner's expression of joy come over Robyn's face.

Robyn had learned about these new plans from a friend who was part of a Christian business group that met each month to share opportunities and experiences running their companies as stewards of God's business. She was initially skeptical that this approach to reducing health care expenses might somehow hurt or not be of interest to her employees, even though the case studies sounded convincing. **The upfront deductible approach should work well for all types of businesses, school districts, government workers and non-profits, she concluded, even though many of us tend to focus on short term desires and expectations versus longer term opportunities.**

Robyn was frustrated that the company's current plan cost too much and that payroll contributions were too high. An Upfront Deductible plan with an HRA/FSA or HSA option seemed like a reasonable way to maintain quality health benefits and increase net take-home pay by reducing employee per pay deductions.

The overall concept also fell in line with her mantra, "The 5 Ps", which stands for **"Prior Planning Promotes Positive Performance"**. Ann's interest re-enforced her decision to give this new approach a try.

It made sense to Robyn that insurance company losses drop when the insurer does not pay claim dollars until a $2,500 to $5,000 deductible is satisfied. She also agreed that exposing the actual cost of health care services to her employees might help them become part of the solution to controlling rising premiums. Offering to pay the first half of the deductible made the plan more palatable as it offers 100% coverage up to a threshold.

The potential savings were appealing enough that some of her management group had recommended dropping the copay plan and only offering the new plan. In the end, Robyn, her CFO and the Vice President of Human Resources agreed that such a step was too radical for their culture.

Robyn also knew that she must enroll in and promote the new Upfront Deductible plan. The tougher decision for her was whether to sign up for the HRA and FSA, or save money in the HSA. She liked that the new program included three plan options, and that reasons to start an HSA differ from choosing the HRA.

With one child still in high school and another in college, she and her former husband expected college tuition payments to continue for another six years. Robyn was only covering herself at this point, and had fortunately enjoyed good health, except for a back problem from an auto accident that knocked her to her knees every so often. At age 45 she could deposit at least $2,000 on top of the $1,250 provided by the company into an HSA. She also knew that she had the option to use the HSA funds to pay pre-tax for all the same products and services available in an FSA.

Since she could afford the potential cash flow risk of the HSA and was intrigued about maximizing retirement savings, she ultimately decided it made the most sense. **It was also nice that HSAs allow for self-substantiation so all she had to do was batch together her receipts and hold on to them for six years if ever personally audited by the IRS.**

She had been advised that most employers provide less money for an HSA than they promise in an HRA. In the end, the committee decided the right decision was to offer the same amount for both HRA and HSA, minimizing confusion and helping promote a long term health care retirement savings philosophy. Although 20 year's older, Robyn's chart mirrored Ann's. Robyn was glad for the counsel of her Christian peers that led her to awareness that accepting reasonable risk for future savings means winning the health care game.

Current Plan:	$2,600 in payroll deductions
	$ 600 in expected copays
	$3,200 KNOWN COST
Additional risk:	$4,400 to out of pocket cap
Max Exposure	**$7,600**
New Plan:	$1,300 in payroll deductions
	$0 in deductible
	$1,300 KNOWN COST
Additional risk:	$3,750 to out of pocket cap
Total	**$5,050**
Expected Savings:	*$1,900*
Worst Case Savings:	*$2,250*

XV. *Young Bev & Barry's Family Challenge*

It is a crazy existence being in your 30's with 5 young children under the age of 10. Bev was tired every morning even if the lights went out by 10:00 pm every night. The twin boys and their sister, who was only 11 months younger, had to be fed by 7:00 am in order to make the bus to school. Barry dropped them off at the corner on his way to work.

Bev had almost an hour after the older ones left to get the babies, now 2 and 3 years old, ready for day care. Drop off was at 8:30 am, fortunately right near her office.

She had been trying to shed the weight from bearing children, but it seemed impossible. Besides the cakes, cookies and doughnuts that were almost always available at work, she did not like coffee and was used to drinking soda throughout the day as a pick up. The sugar and caffeine combination was effective, though short term.

Her doctor had informed her about an increasing risk for diabetes if she did not lose up to 40 pounds. Her glucose level had surpassed the magic 100 milliliter mark. It worried her, so when she tried dieting, it included switching to sugar free soda and a starvation ritual. Bev also walked for 20 minutes with Ann during their lunch break if the weather cooperated, although this was the extent of Bev's formal exercise routine.

Having the best health insurance was a major reason she had gone back to work. Since her parents both had cancer operations requiring hospitalization, she worried if heredity meant she was destined in the future to fight cancer herself. Barry worked for a large, national company that offered plan choices, but they overcharged for family coverage. With her job, she could cover herself and the children for much less in payroll deductions. He covered just himself, and never seemed to get sick.

Always looking to save money, she decided after discussing the option with Ann that it was worth the analysis to consider the new Upfront Deductible option, even though it included a $5,000 family deductible. She understood the HRA and FSA since these plan options were offered by her husband's company. Most of their day care costs and medical copays were already paid pre-tax.

FSA - How much to save?

FSA expense costs $300 and your tax rate = 30%

Without an FSA	With an FSA
You must make **$429** in gross income	You only need **$300** in gross income to pay it.

$129 lost to taxes

Bev's chart of premium savings versus payment risk looked as follows:

Current Plan:	$5,000 in payroll deductions
	$1,500 in expected copays
	$6,700 KNOWN COST
Additional risk:	$8,500 to the out of pocket cap
Max Exposure:	**$15,000**
New Plan:	$2,800 in payroll deductions
	$2,500 in deductible
	$5,500 KNOWN COST
Additional risk:	$5,000 to out of pocket cap
Max Exposure:	**$12,800**
Expected Savings:	*$1,200*
Worst Case Savings:	*$2,200*

Premium savings supported making the switch, taking the HRA and deferring $2,500 into the FSA. Since the change was simply financial and did not impact their choice of providers, plus included 100% catastrophic protection for the children and her, to her it made sense. But she wasn't sure it was worth the hassle with all of the other responsibilities on their plate. In the end she would defer money into the FSA so that at least their copays would now be paid with pre-tax dollars using the Debit Card.

101

What should we look for in a quality health insurance plan? It starts by confirming that hospitals, doctors and pharmacies allow geographical ease to receive services in network. Next consider the amount of freedom you desire when receiving medical care, and what is your risk tolerance. Do you mind getting an approval to be covered for a visit with the heart specialist? If not, then maybe an HMO is right for you. There may be enough other hassles in your life that dealing with health care reimbursements is of no interest.

XVI. *Invincible Charlie's Winning Choice*

Charlie believed Americans have the freedom to make choices, including whether or not to be insured for health care needs. He considered health insurance a luxury of our advanced society, even though others see purchasing health insurance as an American responsibility.

While financially inefficient for the cost of office visits to be pre-paid by insurance premiums, the routine is established with the birth of a child. Scheduled visits to confirm growth progress are "pre-paid". Pediatricians chart growth patterns, administer immunizations and measure reactions. A healthy child experiences additional follow up care once teething infuriates the nasal passages. Nostril ooze may or may not mean there is a bacterial or viral condition. Young parents often visit the doctor to be certain their baby is healthy and comfortable.

The pattern of "running" to the doctor has begun. Unfortunately some children first are exposed to viruses and bacterium while playing with toys in the doctor's waiting room. Prescriptions to fight these microbes necessitate follow up visits and more exposure.

As we age, decisions for elective health care procedures can lead to unexpected illness. The risk of infection should be a major consideration when deciding about a hip or knee replacement. Simple logic, like avoiding hospitals in the winter months reduces the potential for post-operative infections. Recycled air exposure is a reality especially when the heat is on.

If we have limited or no consideration for the cost of a health care purchase because it is paid in full by insurance or society, our sensibilities about return on investment become skewed and lead to "use abuse". When knowledge about total cost is a factor, personal acceptance of the entire burden, both financial and physical is more likely to occur.

And then you have young guys like Charlie who believe they do not need health insurance. Why reduce their pay for protection when they rarely get sick? Clinics and hospitals can't turn anyone away is the thinking. At age 25 and accomplished in a variety of sports, Charlie especially loved skiing and club soccer.

Not being insured was risky, but so is life the way he looked at it. Charlie had historically declined health insurance coverage to have extra money for his sports adventures.

He was aware that with the new Obamacare law he could be fined or taxed for not being insured, but he had also heard that the penalty was less expensive than insurance he might never use and would be collected by reducing his tax refund.

REALITY AS A WAKE UP CALL
It was the story about a buddy who wiped out on his bike and hit a tree that shocked him into thinking about

signing up for health insurance. Charlie's friend got banged up so badly that after two operations, including a titanium rod inserted into his femur, he ended up out of work for six months. His friend did not have health insurance and was now paying $250 per month for the next 10 years to pay off the cost of his care.

Ultimately he concluded that a plan that cost the fewest dollars had some appeal, should he ever crash after jumping off his favorite cliff at Snowbird® in Utah, even if it meant one less ski adventure. Here is his chart which Ann kindly prepared for him as he reminded her of her younger brother.

Current Plan:	$0 in payroll deductions
	$0 in expected copays
	$0 KNOWN COST
Additional risk:	*EVERYTHING!*
New Plan:	$1,300 in payroll deductions
	$0 in deductible
	$1,300 KNOWN COST
Additional risk:	$3,750 to out of pocket cap
Total	**$5,050**
Expected Savings:	*Peace of Mind*
Worst Case Savings:	*No Comparison*

If people have to choose between spending money on food or medicine, the system is broken. This notion is often reviewed in news stories to reinforce that access to quality health care is a right. So then, what level of risk exposure is reasonable? The Affordable Care Act tells us just over $6,000 is about right.

The right health insurance plan should balance payroll deductions with one's ability to afford medical services. Financial efficiency is about thresholds, including what we can and cannot afford to spend from take-home pay and savings.

Take your own test by adding up what you and your family anticipate spending for health care needs. If the amount is significant and future expenses will continue to be high, a plan with low copays and high premiums may be best for you.

Upfront Deductible plans offer premium savings versus copay plans for accepting risk, which is easy to remember and can be neutralized. Their simplicity in design enhances why they are the best coverage to win the health care game over time.

Sample Health Insurance Risk Analysis

Your Current Plan: $_____ in payroll deductions

$_____ in expected copays

$_____ KNOWN COST

Additional risk: $_____ to out of pocket cap

Max Exposure: **$_____**

New Plan: $_____ in payroll deductions

$_____ in deductible

$_____ KNOWN COST

Additional risk: $_____ to out of pocket cap

Max Exposure: **$_____**

Expected Savings: _____

Worst Case Savings: _____

Effectively Winning the Health Care Game

XVII. Bargained Plans & Too Much Insurance

Unionized labor earns credit as a major force behind the founding of America's employer funded health insurance system. Wage controls to minimize inflation during World War II prompted bargaining for employer paid hospitalization. Winning this benefit for workers served America well then and confirmed the standard for employers investing in the health of its workers.

Now, only a few generations later, this laudable success is at the center of our ever increasing affordability problem. Little or no out-of-pocket cost insurance coverage to treat ailments is considered the gold standard. When available to patients an ever increasing volume of services and procedures are performed hyper inflating claims costs leading to unsustainable premium increases.

Health care products and services relieve pain, neutralize symptoms and at times, especially in complex and sophisticated situations, are curative. The diagnosis of worrisome symptoms, especially for parents concerned for their children, is a priceless benefit. Health insurance is important so that if at some point in the future a loved one becomes ill, financial protection exists to cover the cost of health care treatment.

Evidence Based Medicine studies conclude that as much as half of health care services Americans receive are not clinically necessary. People will use more health care if out of pocket costs are nominal. More services do not necessarily make us healthier. Health care providers act more defensively, motivated by malpractice concerns or profit if insurance pays the bills. If it doesn't personally cost us much, why not be certain and order all of the tests possible?

Well-intentioned union leaders bargain away wage increases to maintain rich health insurance benefits. Since decision makers are usually older than the average union member, the personal importance of generous coverage may be greatest to them and their spouses. Couple this with how our society focuses on short term desires and expectations. These end up being barriers to embracing the advantages longer term opportunities.

Younger members today will need more health care later, so fairness is not at issue. When bargaining includes funding Health Savings Accounts as a future standard, more members will be better served with costs not rising as quickly, and pre-tax efficiency in the purchase of health care services increasing net take home pay.

The following charts that show how pre-tax health care savings can grow even when funds are used every year for normal and at times high cost health care needs. No worker should be denied this opportunity as they are then shut out from winning the health care game.

HEALTH SAVINGS ACCOUNT GROWTH PROJECTION
INDIVIDUAL COVERAGE

AGE	DEPOSITS	USAGE	NET GROWTH @ 5%
45	$2,500	$1,500	$1,050
46	$2,500	$1,500	$2,153
47	$2,500	$1,500	$3,310
48	$2,500	$1,500	$4,526
49	$2,500	$1,500	$5,802
50	$3,000	$3,000	$6,092
51	$3,000	$1,750	$7,709
52	$3,000	$1,750	$9,407
53	$3,000	$1,750	$11,190
54	$3,000	$1,750	$13,062
55	$3,500	$3,500	$13,715
56	$3,500	$2,000	$15,976
57	$3,500	$2,000	$18,350
58	$3,500	$2,000	$20,842
59	$3,500	$2,000	$23,459
60	$4,000	$4,000	$24,632
61	$4,000	$2,500	$27,439
62	$4,000	$2,500	$30,386
63	$4,000	$2,500	$33,480
64	$4,000	$2,500	$36,729
65	$5,000	$5,000	$38,565
66	$5,000	$3,000	$42,594
67	$5,000	$3,000	$46,823
68	$5,000	$3,000	$51,264
69	$6,000	$6,000	$53,828

Assumes 5% compound interest earnings & maximum projected deferrals.

111

HEALTH SAVINGS ACCOUNT GROWTH PROJECTION
COVERAGE WITH DEPENDENTS

AGE	DEPOSITS	USAGE	NET GROWTH @ 5%
45	$5,000	$2,000	$3,150
46	$5,000	$2,000	$6,458
47	$5,000	$2,000	$9,930
48	$5,000	$2,000	$13,577
49	$5,000	$2,000	$17,406
50	$6,000	$6,000	$18,276
51	$6,000	$2,250	$23,127
52	$6,000	$2,250	$28,221
53	$6,000	$2,250	$33,570
54	$6,000	$2,250	$39,186
55	$7,000	$7,000	$41,145
56	$7,000	$2,500	$47,927
57	$7,000	$2,500	$55,049
58	$7,000	$2,500	$62,526
59	$7,000	$2,500	$70,377
60	$8,000	$8,000	$73,896
61	$8,000	$3,000	$82,841
62	$8,000	$3,000	$92,233
63	$8,000	$3,000	$102,095
64	$8,000	$3,000	$112,450
65	$9,000	$9,000	$118,072
66	$9,000	$4,000	$129,226
67	$9,000	$4,000	$140,937
68	$9,000	$4,000	$153,234
69	$10,000	$10,000	$160,895

Assumes 5% compound interest earnings & maximum projected deferrals.

XVIII. Charge Master Woes &
The Need for Reform

Billing reform has not been effectively addressed in the PPACA law. Insurance companies negotiate discounts that can equal as much as much as 80% below the "charge" for a medical supply or service. Waiting weeks following a medical procedure to learn the charge and its discounted cost is common. Invoices patients receive are confusing. Arguments offered by health care professionals to justify the current system are bluntly bogus.

Real price transparency must expand to win the health care game, increasing awareness of the actual cost of health care services. This will allow patients to better consider the true value of services.

Insurance companies, doctors and hospitals have defended the importance of keeping private the details of secretive pricing agreements in the spirit of adhering to laws against price collusion and monopolization. While this risk exists with transparency, an opportunity for price competition is also engaged.

Maintaining a charge master (or charges roster) is a health care provider's obligation. Medicare originally paid providers a discounted amount determined from the charge master. The original Medicare payment approach was replaced in time by a flat fee system, but the obligation to maintain a charge master, or price list, continued and is used as a tool for setting discounts with private insurance companies, along with over charging the uninsured.

Inflated charges lead to outrageous discounts. Like a proverbial shell game, this pricing approach is similar to the Oriental rug store offering an 80% discount every day of the year. There is no truth to their "full price" claim. Retailers slash real prices only when going out of business. In health care, high discount levels are used by insurers to showcase their "negotiating efficiency" versus competitors. Winners are seeing through this charade.

Think about a $160 charge for a $100 service equating to a 38% discount. Increase the charge to $175 while continuing to accept $100 and the discount jumps to 57%. No additional value is achieved except the perception of a higher discount percentage. The charge for a physician office visit may be $200 with the insurance company approving $120, or 60% of the charge. THIS IS CRAZY!

Patients have been known to conclude that their physicians are being "ripped off" by insurance companies when bills are heavily discounted. Such thinking is as corrupt as the charge master itself.

American health care's contorted payment approach benefits no one in the end, since services seem more expensive than they truly are. It also feeds a negative paradigm that prompts many

patients to ignore bills from providers, adding to payment delinquency.

Although higher costs are often translated to mean greater value, the opposite can also be true. It should cost less to have an operation by a team of professionals who performs specific procedures repeatedly. Efficiencies in quality and cost will increasingly emerge with price transparency.

Consolidated, bundled billing for services and procedures may ultimately replace line by line "fee for service" billing standards due to PPACA. Comparison of cost may then become available based on quality, value and price, which is a standard in other businesses.

With the current charges master system and discount variability, true costs for care are often as clear as mud. Replacement with a transparent pricing approach including mark ups versus what Medicare pays is just one idea to reform the system. Winning the health care game must include fundamental billing reform.

Actual Charges & Discounts in 2012

Service	Charge	Approved	Discount
A. MRI	$ 1,803.00	$ 676.13	63%
B. Office	$ 313.00	$ 198.89	36%
C. Inpatient	$41,926.00	$15,722.25	62%
D. X-Ray	$ 398.00	$ 177.90	45%

XIX. Accepting Our "Wonderfully Simple" Health Insurance System

When traditional deductible and coinsurance plans were replaced by low out-of-pocket HMO, POS and PPO plans, premiums ultimately rose at a rate significantly greater than inflation. Increases were in part because of laws like COBRA and HIPAA that extended access to employer provided coverage when workers resigned or were terminated. Pre-existing condition exclusions for new hires and family members were also eliminated with these well designed laws, as long as insurance had not terminated for more than a two month period of time.

These protections eliminated the need to cover a spouse and children under more than one employer sponsored plan. If a spouse lost their job they legally became eligible to enroll as a dependent under their spouse's plan without delay or penalty.

As fewer workers maintained double coverage, less money to cover health insurance premium was paid to insurers, further escalating rate hikes.

KEEPING IT SIMPLE

The early success of HMOs had confirmed American appreciation for preventive health care protection and no paperwork hassles. Rising premiums were an acceptable tradeoff for quite some time, before value sensitivity began to shift following years of double digit premium increases.

Prior to HMOs gaining market share, a popular health insurance plan offered the same simplicity and was sold by The Guardian Life Insurance Company. This era preceded Managed Care, meaning there weren't formal health care provider networks with the exception of regional Blue Cross and Blue Shield agreements with doctors and hospitals. Simple copays for office visits and prescriptions were yet to be invented.

The Guardian plan was called the "$100 deductible, 100% plan". It was simple and comprehensive. Some might ask why it wasn't simply a "100%" coverage plan. The answer lies in the relative value of $100 back then, plus understanding how to limit rapid insurance premium cost escalation.

Calculating the value of compound inflation and moving forward a generation, the purchasing value of $100 then is similar to $1,000 today. Self-insuring the first $1,000 eliminates paying claims for a majority of the people insured.

The Guardian plan's popularity ultimately dwindled as the $100 deductible barrier became eroded by inflation. HMO, PPO and POS plans also took hold as nominal copays for office visits became preferred, even if at a limited network of doctors.

The evolution of HMOs impacted every American. This well intentioned concept effectively eliminated patient consideration for the cost of health care services. The "numbing down" that occurred, where patients began to believe office visit and prescriptions only cost the $10 copay they paid, contributed to dramatic increases in health care use and unaffordable premiums.

GOING FULL CIRCLE
Consumer Driven Health Care Plans (CDHPs) evolved in the first decade of the 21st Century as a full circle return to upfront deductible insurance plans like the once popular Guardian "$100 deductible, 100% plan".

With upfront deductible plans, transparency as to the real cost of health care services is reality. Patients are financially motivated to learn prices for elective health care services. Government approval for plan designs that promote learning about the actual health care costs was affirmed with the creation of HRAs & HSAs.

Plans with $1,000 or more in Upfront Deductibles are now the standard at more than 50% of small employers, according to Dr. Drew Altman, CEO of the Kaiser Family Foundation.

PARADIGM SHIFT
When is enough of something too much? In our technologically progressive culture, this diabolical issue creeps into almost everything. Enriched wheat flour,

high fructose corn syrup and hydrogenated oils are great products, but they have their downside when it comes to potential weight gain. Sport Utility Vehicles (SUVs) are versatile, but burn more fuel than four door sedans. Awareness of relative value and the unintended consequences of perceived progress emerge over time.

For many years caring employers paid most health care expenses. The government eases this burden by making premiums a tax-deductible business expense.

Health coverage should be comprehensive, protecting us like a warm wool blanket on a cold night, minimizing financial exposure. Concerns are common that the more financial responsibility we accept ends up reducing necessary care provided to maintain good health and leading to an increase in catastrophically expensive care down the road.

An alternative perspective is that judicious consumers will purchase what is needed and not just what may appear desirable or recommended. Employers have been making these tough insurance coverage decisions on behalf of employees, spurning acceptance by workers relieved when payroll deductions no longer rise.

For defensive medicine reasons, at times doctors will suggest additional tests "just to be sure." Smart consumers learn to ask if a test is necessary now, or convenient for protecting against low percentage absolutes.

The automobile industry has had to adapt to increased consumer awareness of a vehicle's wholesale cost versus it sales price. Hospitals, doctors and pharmaceutical companies will hopefully reform their charges and billing philosophy as consumer's demand cost transparency.

Businesses pay health insurance premiums to maintain workforce efficiency, expecting that insurance will cover all the bills for catastrophic health events. Employer interest in a healthy work force is based coldly on maximizing productivity.
An efficient system balances coverage levels with affordable premiums. Acceptance of payment risk to offset premium increases is a growing reality, part of the paradigm shift.

Phenomenal advancements in medicine are extending life spans, increasing quality of life standards, reducing discomfort and pain, and curing ailments, but there is no free lunch. Low copay HMOs could not survive ongoing premium rate increases. The Affordable Care Act underscores this reality with what is known as the "Cadillac Tax", adding a 40% surcharge on premiums that exceed a threshold as of 2018.

2014	FSA	HRA	HSA
First available	1978	2002	2004
Funding	Flexible	Employer	Flexible
Plan Design	n/a	n/a	QHDHP
Max Deferral	$2,500	n/a	$3,300 S/ $6,550F
Catch up option	n/a	n/a	$1,000 ages 55+
Maximum Out-of-Pocket	n/a	n/a	$6,350 Single $12,700 Family
Rollover	2.5 months	Employer	Unlimited
Interest accrual	n/a	Employer	Yes
Portability	No	No	Yes
Taxation	Pre-Tax	Pre-Tax	Pre-Tax
Section 213d	Yes	Yes	Yes
Retiree Premium & LTC	No	Yes	Medicare Advantage & LTC

XX. The Economics of Health Care & Health Care Employment

"Venture Capital Delivers $110 million for Advancing Spine Correction Therapies." "Hospital Drives Local Economy as the Largest Regional Employer." "The Average Senior Citizen will spend $200,000 on Health Care Needs Post Retirement." "Pharmaceutical Companies Invest $300 million Developing a New Blockbuster Drug." "President Obama proposes $100 billion in research grants to eradicate memory loss for aging Americans".

Headlines like these in our newspapers appear with some frequency. Health care is a specialty topic for many writers and investment managers.

This is big business! As expenditures grow, normally price efficiency results. This has yet to occur with health care. Our willingness to pay more and more for the latest health care innovation is supported by how insurance works. Shouldn't we assume that a $10,000 procedure to reduce back pain is less effective than the new $20,000 alternative?

Research and development is incentivized by the desire to make a profit along with increasing quality of life. Health care consumers are hardly able to react to true value. Collective costs spin out of control in the name of progress.

WHO MAKES THE DECISION
Our government collects so much in taxes earmarked for health care that it is the largest single payor to hospitals. But the government does not purchase actual health care services. It is the physician community and each of us that purchase health care services. The government and insurance companies are the third party payor for what we purchase.

Government mandates to insurance companies are designed to be in our collective best interest, ensuring our health care needs are covered.

Everyone desires the best health and immediate help when suffering. Affordability of health care is one of the greatest challenges of our modern era.

ACCOUNTABLE CARE ORGANIZATIONS
Who is included in a list of the largest employers in your community? Look it up and you will find hospitals at or near the top. Hospitals always seem to be building a new wing or parking garage. Medical buildings fill up with physician practices in spite of a nursing or doctor shortage.

Economically, health care spending is important for providing all kinds of jobs. Colleges and universities benefit financially from training students to be future health care workers. Construction firms benefit from building new hospitals. Building suppliers benefit from providing the materials to build these facilities. And now all new hospitals are constructed with private rooms to reduce infection rates.

The new term for networks of hospitals and doctor groups is ACO or Accountable care Organization. As demand for services potentially outpaces supply until the aging baby boom generation passes on, these institutions will continue to challenge expectations for efficiency.

By 2030 it is projected there will be 80 million Americans covered by Medicare, almost doubling its size in one half of a generation. Since baby boomers are living longer than their parents, a fall-off in demand may not occur until 2050. Even with the good news that so many of us are living longer because we receive great health care, where is the affordability tipping point?

Will we continue to invest greater resources in health care to promote job growth and overall quality of life? Let's get personal. What would you do if you knew a possible cure existed for your problem and it was only a matter of money to enhance your chance for full recovery? This is a rhetorical question to reflect on why we will continue to see the business of health care grow. It is only a bad thing if our society declines in other ways because we devote excessive resources to health care.

THE ROLE OF GOVERNMENT

Legislators and policy makers affect health care in this country in many ways, including the formation of laws impacting taxation of health care and payments for health care services under Medicare and Medicaid.

Government initiatives also fund the advancement of our population's quality of health. It is a complex responsibility. The HMO Act of 1973 was approved at the end of the Nixon administration. It took ten years for the concept to become popular, but once accepted, health coverage changed for most Americans by reducing out of pocket risk.

The Affordable Care Act includes goals for fixing our health care system by eliminating redundancies and making electronic medical records that track details increase the standard for efficiency.

Concerns exist that private health care information will be improperly shared once all records are electronic, plus while we might not have to pay much out of pocket for care we may wait an extended period of time to be treated for chronic conditions. This is the dominant complaint in Great Britain and Canada. The necessity to "wait" seems counter intuitive to our free market system.

Patient awareness of the financial impact of health care decisions may efficiently balance utilization levels and avoid rationing. This will mean real progress has been made for winning the health care game.

XXI. Prescriptions & the Growth of Over-the-Counter Products & Therapies

Prescription Rx costs make up between 15% - 25% of health insurance premiums. New prescription therapies are termed "wonder drugs" with their impact on enhancing quality of life. Heart transplants are on the decline thanks to new medicines that assist a diseased heart to work with greater efficiency. Wow, that is progress!

The abbreviation "Rx" comes from the Latin word "recipere" and means "to take". The English language synonym is our word recipe. A prescription is an order to take a certain medicine. Medicines are compounds of various chemicals.

Prescription Rx coverage receives tremendous attention because of the ever growing number of curative compounds available. There seem to be as many medicines to choose from as there are mutual funds! More and more medications are formulated for long-term usage. A good allergy medication used daily can dramatically improve one's quality of life. Winners at the health care game take their medicine, adhering to doctor's orders.

WATCH OUT!

Prescriptions are high potency "controlled substances" if they require a doctor's approval for purchase. Ingested in very small amounts, medicines are a concentrated mixture of chemicals designed to affect one's body function. Prescription compounds can be poisonous if consumed in excess. Certain medications should not be consumed with other medicines and supplements as they can induce dangerous side effects.

Dosages prescribed vary depending upon the condition of the patient, their age, body mass and gender. Often an originally prescribed dose may be reduced as a health condition improves. This question should be asked at every office visit by winners of the health care game who take chronic care medications.

Physicians and pharmacists may offer advice whether there are Over-The-Counter (OTC) products to improve our medical conditions. Winners of the health care game know that many over the counter products were at one time prescription medicines, and can be paid for pre-tax from HSA & FSA funds if a doctor writes a prescription. Examples include Claritin®, Zyrtec® and Prilosec®.

PATENT PROTECTION
Entrepreneurial scientists receive venture capital funding and invest years of research and millions of dollars to discover safe and effective prescription Rx compounds. A 17 year patent on a blockbuster medicine allows for charges of $5.50 or more per pill for a medicine that once off patent may be sold at a reasonable profit for half of that amount.

Pharmaceutical innovation in the development of treatments that prevent and cure maladies are supported by the United States government with grants of long term patent protection so that development costs can be recovered.

Frustration is common when a "single source" drug a doctor prescribes is expensive. The ability to charge a high cost allows the innovator to recover the research investment associated with all the phases of development culminating in obtaining a patent for a curative medicine.

Patients who believe they are overcharged for controlled substances should inquire if there are lower cost alternatives with adequate effectiveness. Decisions that include patients not filling their prescriptions or taking half doses to save money are an unintended reality in this age of expensive medicine costs. It is a real life conundrum.

Proponents of patent protection agree that many medicines would not be discovered without the patent system. Since competitors are not allowed to manufacture and sell the same prescription Rx until the patent has expired, concern exists of price gouging the consumer.

One of the most popular medicines ever invented to treat high cholesterol, Lipitor, lost its patent protection in 2011. The medicine generated more than $10 billion in annual sales. Competing generic alternatives are now reducing costs for this Rx, with certain retailers marketing a free supply of the generic to induce patients to switch. This marketplace efficiency is healthy.

COMPLEX PRICING TERMINOLOGY

The actual production cost of many medicines can be dramatically less than their retail price. Distribution pricing schemes include selling medicines at a discount below the Average Wholesale Price (AWP). As a term, AWP is a misnomer and has been challenged in the courts. A drug must be significantly marked up to the Average Wholesale Price in order to sell it at AWP minus 15% - 70%. Prescription Benefit Managers (PBMs) use this terminology along with acronyms like MAC (Maximum Allowable Cost) when establishing Rx prices. The latest pricing acronym to emerge is WAC (Wholesale Acquisition Cost). Like the charge master in a hospital, overly complex pricing schemes add to complexity and cost. A change to "Cost Plus" pricing lowers prices paid by patients and is more transparent.

IMPACT ON PATIENTS

When Rx copayments remain flat for multiple years, a smaller and smaller percentage of the cost of a medicine is paid by patients assuming the cost of the medicine rises with inflation. Awareness of this reality has prompted the introduction of percentage (%) cost sharing. Price awareness can be an asset for patients paying a percentage of the cost of a medicine versus flat copays, prompting questions to physicians about dosage levels and alternative therapies.

Medicines may be offered as "loss leaders" to attract customers. Retailers who market generic prescriptions for copays of $4.00 per fill are acquiring medicines at the true wholesale, or acquisition cost. Low copays for generic drugs prompt shoppers to buy medicines and other products while at the retailer's store.

Monthly pharmacy refills are inconvenient and higher in cost for patients on chronic care brand medications. Mail order Rx purchases reduce the end user's cost through lower prices than medicines stocked at retail pharmacies. Saving one monthly copayment is an effective inducement to receive three months of medicine delivered by mail. Turn around for delivery averages less than one week.

Non-narcotic medications are becoming increasingly available for purchase at physician offices and clinics, plus with Tele-medicine physicians. Important to note is that these approaches negate the value of speaking face to face with expert pharmacists.

The real cost of medicines is the patient's responsibility if participating in a qualified High Deductible Health Plan (HDHP), since prescriptions are subject to the upfront deductible. Once the deductible has been satisfied, prescription copays generally are the patient's responsibility. So the $5.50 per day pill costs $2,000 per year and is paid pre-tax dollars to win the health care game.

XXII. Diseases & Syndromes, Chronic & Acute

Winning the health care game includes recognizing and planning for the reality that we all ultimately will have something wrong with our health. It is a question of when, not if.

Certain problems last a lifetime, like dry skin. Osgood-Schlatter disease sounds horrible. Like Alzheimer's disease, it is named for the person who isolated the condition. Unlike Alzheimer's, Osgood-Schlatter is a buildup of calcium below the knee cap that is painful to the fast growing junior high school athlete, often leaving the knees weakened for life.

Syndromes are multiple symptoms that characterize a disease or abnormality. Symptoms are abnormal circumstances, like a rash or a cough that may be indicators of a greater abnormality. Disease is a condition that impairs normal functioning. Chronic conditions are ongoing, like diabetes and certain cancers, while acute conditions occur rapidly and are intense. A broken bone and hypothermia are acute conditions.
The common cold is a syndrome that transitions from being an acute to a chronic condition. It is also a short term disease.

Illness, injury, pain, disability and death are all part of the life experience. Medicines that help to cure one ailment can result in additional conditions and side effects. Science and technological advances in

133

health care improve living conditions for every generation.

New disease isolation developed rapidly in the twentieth century. Older people are aware of the term "consumption." Many in the 19th century died with this all inclusive term as the cause. It is no longer used today because science and medicine so effectively pin points the root cause of ill health.

Unfortunately, diagnoses are not always accurate. Some can also negatively impact how we look at life and affect our hopes and dreams. A doctor's diagnosis, sometimes when delivered in the Latin form may negatively impact our sense of the future. And yet, mind over body stories exist that are awe inspiring. Often diseases result in only short term discomfort. The aches and pains of life are part of the experience. Some are intense, some bearable and some self-inflicted, like obesity or a hangover.

"Hypochondriac" is one of our best understood multi-syllabic terms. It is reality that all of us live with varying levels of discomfort. How we treat ourselves physically and emotionally offers the greatest impact on our quality of life. Even sick people smile, sending heartwarming messages to the rest of us.

Conditions like leukemia, a form of blood cancer, are too often a death sentence. Many of the deadliest conditions are labeled as cancer, striking down people at all ages. Cancer is a disease, and because there are so many types and stages, some die quickly while others live a long time once diagnosed and treated. Curative health care treatment based upon scientific principles can be an inspired art form.

It is up to us who plan on winning the health care game to take it all in stride and be realistic about expectations for how to live a quality life. Our choices end up being impacted by financial reality but are mostly emotional and spiritual.

XXIII. The New Way to Ask Your Doctor

Winners at the health care game think about how many doctor's office visits are diagnostic and curative, along with what percentage of the time a trip to the doctor is an "assurance" visit. Monitoring by physicians is important to a good cure and asking your doctor questions may be critical to the discovery the root cause. So it comes down being sensible to avoid redundancy.

Our physicians are licensed and trained to effectively "spend" health care dollars. They order tests, determine conditions and prescribe treatment solutions. Trusting them allows for the isolation of medical problems plus their correction and cure. Physicians are regarded as our brightest and most talented citizens.

Physician training is really expensive. Unlike most other Western nations where the government funds the cost of medical school, personal financing of tuition in America can lead to debt that is so high, repayment schedules last as long as a home mortgage.

Being a doctor is an intellectually challenging and often uncomfortable career, especially for care givers assisting patients at the end of their lives.

Doctors must be business people in order to thrive financially. They negotiate with families and hospital administrators, often working long hours in service to their patients. We expect these professionals to recommend solutions that maximize the quality of our health and we also expect them to be perfect.

Do doctors want 100% of the care they provide to be paid by insurance? Sit in a crowded primary care physician waiting room and consider how physicians transition from one patient to the next. They are not distracted by whether the patient or their health plan is paying the bill. Ultimately they know that most of the cost of running their practice will be paid through insurance plan payments. They appropriately delegate these details to professional office administrators.

Self-pay is not common. It can be difficult to collect fees from patients who pay for care themselves. As self-pay increases, the number of visits for the average patient declines. Logic follows that demand for services is a function of need and personal cost responsibility. Doctors understand that the demand for health care services increases as more people are covered by insurance.

The trend toward concierge medicine where patients pay fees upfront to physicians who then reduce the number of people they serve is a proven way to ensure prompt and immediate attention. It is a luxury for those with the means to pay for it.

America needs our physicians to help control the growth in health care expenses. We encumber them with significant malpractice concerns and insurance premiums, promoting defensive medicine approaches and higher fees. There can be a fine line between malpractice and mal-occurrence. Reasonable non-economic award caps should become a national standard to protect against mistreatment, while at the same time paying for mistakes when care or the lack of it harms patients.

Patient Awareness of the Actual Cost of Health Care Services Reduces Defensive Medicine Spending, Translating into Double Digit Premium Savings.

XXIV. "High Volume, Low Cost" Copays

Winning the health care game can include taking steps that reflect logical compromise. Since health care consumers and providers are used to copays as a payment standard, it makes at times to keep certain financial transactions easy. When a $40 copay is charged at the end of an office visit or completing a prescription purchase transaction, simplicity reigns.

Since rising health care expenses have prompted health insurers to increase copays for higher cost services, including hospitalization, outpatient procedures, X-rays, and laboratory services, it hurts patients pockets more, but still masks the true cost of care. These copays still offset a minor portion of the true cost of health care services. Copays exacerbate the overall cost awareness conundrum since often patients do not know or care to grasp what an insignificant portion of the overall cost of care their copay represents.

While the Federal government approved qualified HDHP designs that subject all diagnostic health care services to deductibles, these plans can be complicated to some of us. In addition, the high deductible responsibility coupled with lower premiums may leave the impression that HDHPs are of lower quality.

An effective way to increase acceptance of Upfront Deductible plans is a hybrid design that allows patients to continue copays for "high volume, lower cost services" such as office visits and

prescriptions. There is a perceived value advantage versus HDHPs.

An Upfront Deductible plan design that introduces deductibles and coinsurance for low volume, high cost services, while maintaining copays for high volume, low cost services accomplishes the goal of reducing excess utilization of higher cost health care like MRIs, x-ray and lab services, along with elective care.

It also keeps payments simple for highly utilized health care services. These hybrid plans allow for the continuation of copays that have become the contemporary standard, thereby enhancing prescription therapy compliance, positive plan perception and ease of administration.

In order to make changes to the hybrid deductible plan most palatable, employers introducing this type of design often include a Health Reimbursement Arrangement (HRA) to offset a portion of the deductible. The HRA loss ratio averages 15% - 40% of the promised benefit, since office visits and prescriptions are subject to copays. Copays do not qualify for HRA reimbursement.

Upfront Deductible / Copay hybrid plan are well received by patients used to paying copays for office visits and prescriptions. This type of hybrid plan design also does not allow funding of a Health Savings Account.

This plan approach is a valid strategy for self-insured and experienced rated employer groups, but it does fall short for small employers because insurance companies keep 20% of every premium dollar collected plus on average 5% in federal and state taxes. A $150 specialist visit requiring a $50 copay results in a total cost of $175. For the convenience of the insurer mailing $100 to the provider, an extra $25 is added to premiums, about as efficient as parking one's car in a big city lot for an hour. Ouch!

Deductible, Copays & Coinsurance	In NETWORK	Out of NETWORK
Benefits and Services	**Health Reimbursement Account** $1,250 SINGLE / $2,500 FAMILY	
Annual Deductible		
Individual	$2,500	$5,000
Family	$5,000	$10,000
After Deductible Plan Pays	90%	50%
Out of Pocket Limit		
Individual	$5,000	$10,000
Family	$10,000	$20,000
Lifetime Maximum	Unlimited	Unlimited
Preventive Care	100%, no Deductible	50%
Women's Health	100%, no Deductible	50%
Routine Physical	100%, no Deductible	50%
Routine GYN Exam	100%, no Deductible	50%
Well Child Care	100%, no Deductible	50%
Emergency Room	After Deductible, 90%	50%
Physician Office	$25 Copay 100%	50%
Specialist Office	$50 Copay 100%	50%
Chiropractic	$50 Copay 100%	50%
Inpatient Hospital	After Deductible, 90%	50%
Outpatient Hospital	After Deductible, 90%	50%
Maternity	After Deductible, 90%	50%
Surgery and Anesthesia	After Deductible, 90%	50%
Lab / X-Ray	After Deductible, 90%	50%
Physical Therapy	After Deductible, 90%	50%
Inpatient Psychiatric	After Deductible, 90%	50%
Outpatient Psychiatric	After Deductible, 90%	50%
Prescription Drugs	*Prescription Copays*	
Retail Rx	$10 Generic / $40 Preferred / $60 NP	
Mail Order Rx	$25 Generic / $100 Preferred / $150 NP	

XXV. Efficiently Winning the Health Care Game

The savvy will navigate here for reinforcement about winning the health care game. Minimizing premiums by accepting reasonable risk coupled with tax advantaged savings to pay for normal and future health care needs is the winning strategy.

We are evolving to a time when a recommended amount will become a standard for retiree health care savings and regular retirement income savings. Health Savings Accounts will increasingly be promoted alongside 401(k) / 403(b) plans and Individual Retirement Accounts (IRAs).

For Americans lacking the income or desire to save for retirement health care expenses, drawing funds from an HRA and FSA offers efficient short term cash flow protection. These accounts introduce a sense of consumerism, reducing unwarranted health care utilization.

In order to win the health care game pre-tax health care accounts are necessary, married to health care plans with upfront deductibles. Deductibles give consumers pause to evaluate the merits of costly health care services. The logic of the investment becomes self-evident. Tax law allows pre-tax dollars to be used to pay for qualified health care expenses through FSAs, HRAs, and HSAs.

For almost all of us health care service needs are inconsistent over life's tenure. In good times, winners build savings as a bridge for times when there is a need for expensive care.

A qualified High Deductible Health Plan (HDHP) mandates that all services except preventive care are subject to an upfront deductible. Even low cost, high volume services like office visits and prescriptions are subject to deductible satisfaction. Copays and coinsurance may be part of these plans only after the deductible has been paid in full. These HDHPs allow for pre-tax deposits to HSAs. If offered with a deductible offsetting HRA participants cannot also fund an HSA. These choices should be up to the individual.

A popular hybrid design has upfront deductibles for expensive, less often utilized services. Copays are charged for high frequency physician office visits and prescriptions. These plans do not allow legal funding of HSAs, but may include an HRA to offset a portion of deductible responsibility.

"Hospitalization Coverage" evolved as the original name for health insurance, and the term is still in use today. Medicare Part A covers hospitalization expenses, validating its contemporary place. With the addition of coverage for physician services, laboratory, x-ray, office visits and prescriptions, the term "Indemnity Plan" emerged to describe hospitalization plus other health care service coverage. "Traditional Plans" became a default term for Indemnity coverage following the growth in popularity of "Managed Care" insurance which includes Health Maintenance Organization (HMO) plans, Preferred Provider Organization (PPO) and Point of Service (POS) plans. Ultimately PPO plans emerged to be the "New Traditional Plans".

Upfront Deductible Plans are proven to reduce costs resulting in:

- **Lower health care premiums**
- **Lower employee payroll deductions**
- **Pre-tax out of pocket costs**
- **Rollover of unused pre-tax funds**
- **Simplified plan designs**
- **Financial awareness of costs**
- **End to excessive utilization**
- **100% upfront coverage then risk**

So how may an employer and our country introduce the concept of higher deductibles, while maintaining positive morale? For decades individuals recognized that employers and the insurance company "paid their entire health care bill." Now with skyrocketing premiums and ever increasing payroll deductions,

Americans desire to know and limit insurance premium increases. People want to "get what they pay for".

We appreciate having control over our finances and the freedom to make choices. Our savings potential with Upfront Deductible plans occurs after careful analysis of probable utilization of health care services. Utilization is defined as the quantity of health care products purchased and services performed.

An upfront deductible plan offers patients a credible reason to question not the doctor's diagnosis, but the testing or services that may be redundant, able to be procured later, or unnecessary. It also manages a leap of faith that catastrophic health care needs may occur in the future but are not tomorrow's reality.

In addition, the ability to save precious dollars for use on elderly health care costs promotes a lifetime savings desire versus a "use it up" spending mentality. Health care savings are like building equity versus renting. See the savings growth potential on pages 111 & 112.

Value standards for future health insurance purchases can be comparatively explained with an analogy about going out to dinner. The perceived value is different and better at a restaurant with fine service, linen table cloths and expensive entrées. Even though one can end up as full from food delivered through a window wrapped in paper, setting and cost connote lower value.

Nuances of value when dining can be compared with how many of us select a health insurance plan. But times have changed in that government approved coverage requires the same 100%, unlimited health care protection for high cost care regardless of plan choice. Less expensive premium plans are of the same quality except that normal care needs are shifted from an insurance expense to personal responsibility.

Let's review the accounts that offer pre-tax savings:

Health Savings Accounts (HSA) first became available in January 2004, and are now in use by more than 20 million Americans. HSAs require enrollment in a qualified High Deductible Health Plan (HDHP). HSA funds are the personal property of the account owner. Unused funds rollover. To encourage participation an employer may agree to fund a portion of HSAs and promote account owners to contribute their own pre-tax money through a Commitment Contract for building longer term savings. Because HSAs are portable, the funding expense to the business is equal to 100% of the promised benefit.

Flexible Spending Accounts (FSAs) have been available since 1978. This voluntary benefit allows for the pre-tax payment of qualified health care products and services not paid by insurance, saving participants an average of $30 in taxes for every $100 deposited. Deferrals do not rollover to the next year, which limits participation interest. The ability to incur expenses over a 14 ½ month period has enhanced the use of FSAs in recent years, along with awareness that 100% of the annual deferral is available in full at time of need.

Health Reimbursement Arrangement (HRA)

Employers establish a self-insured plan that allows for the reimbursement of qualified medical expenses, and at times with an opportunity to rollover unused amounts. HRA expenses must be entirely funded by the employer and are not portable. Depending upon the plan design and employee turnover, the HRA loss ratio will be 15% to 80% of the promised benefit. The expense to the business is based on how much of the promised benefit is actually used.

WHERE TO GO FROM HERE

To offset double digit premium cost increases, forward thinking employers have adopted "total replacement" Upfront Deductible Plans with the goal of economic beneficence for all participants, including lower income earners. Cost responsibility for one's health care needs must be properly balanced with life's other cost necessities. Upfront Deductible Plans are not meant to expose patients to expenses they cannot meet, but require planning or acceptance of a relative "gusher" cost out lay versus out of pocket costs that "drip" from pay.

Like a frog that slowly boils to its end as the water temperature rises, ever increasing premium costs for low out of pocket insurance plans erode take home pay. With benefits being a form of compensation, including reasonable risk approaches is a winning, responsible course to balance cost and value.

We culturally accept allowing thousands of dollars in spending annually for lower income earners as long as the money "drips" out of out of individual pockets each day. It is the "gusher" expense of thousands of dollars that people with limited funds realistically struggle to afford. When it comes to health care needs, we try to draw the line that risk exposure is wrong minded. This thinking is not logical based upon our inconsistent need for high cost health care services over time.

A proven strategy to meet the needs of participants at various income, cash flow and demographic levels includes offering:

1. A qualified HDHP with the option of HSAs and a <u>Commitment Contract</u> for funding amounts above employer deposits. Employer HSA deposits may be set equal to a projected HRA loss ratio, with half of the annual employer amount funded the first month, and the balance deposited equally over the next 11 months. A limited FSA option is appropriately made available for dental, vision and post deductible medical out of pockets expenses.
2. The same HDHP offered with the option of a first dollar HRA. Participants also have the option to make voluntary deferrals to an FSA. This approach protects cash flow, since 100% of the promised HRA annual FSA deferral is available at time of

need. HRA and FSA funds are conveniently loaded on one Debit Card.

3. A third option at increased payroll contributions is a hybrid Upfront Deductible plan with or without an HRA that includes office visit and prescription Rx copays. Copays are not subject to HRA reimbursement. A voluntary FSA is made available. This approach maintains consumerism for high dollar, lower volume health care services while copays for office visits and prescriptions.

Even though the initial analysis by many human resource and insurance professionals regarding this approach had been that it involves too much change and is not worth the "hassle", sensibilities are maturing. A paradigm shift has taken hold as the approach is now respected for its long term economic efficiency. It is the way to win the health care game.

The trajectory is building for these plans to become the new standard for comprehensive health insurance. Awareness of saving for future retiree health care needs is a welcome derivative of this trend, reducing worry about paying for future health care needs.

The risk avoidance advocates who just don't care and want to keep it all simple with health care needs mostly pre-paid, will hopefully remain able to purchase a new, expensive Cadillac each year. That will be necessary with the 40% surcharge on premiums above a threshold with the "Cadillac Tax". The financial tide is rising against this type of philosophy.

Upfront Deductible Plans and health care consumerism prompts participants to make quality (not quantity) decisions about their medical care needs, increasing fiscal control over health care expense outlays. The cost curve is flattened and pre-tax savings maximized. Results validate the effort as financial health improves without sacrificing personal health. This is how to win the health care game.

"When considering health insurance options, a lower cost premium plan will be BEST when all factors & figures are analyzed & annualized, assuming it includes cash flow protection with the option for building pre-tax savings to pay future health care expense needs."

BENEFITS GLOSSARY

ACCOUNTABLE CARE ORGANIZATION – Terminology describing hospital and physician conglomerates who accept risk in the care of patients, evolving away from fee for service revenue streams

ACQUISITION COST - The true wholesale cost for a health care product; what the provider or reseller pays to the manufacturer

BIO-METRICS – Wellness and prevention information obtained by testing blood, blood pressure, carbon monoxide, nicotine and body mass index

BROKER - Professional representing buyers of insurance rather than insurers

CAFETERIA PLAN – Benefit plan that offers the choice between cash or one or more tax favored options

CHARGE MASTER – A retail price list for all products, services and procedures provided by hospitals and physicians, also referred to as the "charges roster". These prices are dramatically higher than discounted amounts paid by the government and insurance companies

CHIP – Children health insurance plans available from a state

COBRA – Federal law allowing for the continuation of health benefits postemployment for 18 – 36 months, requiring beneficiaries to pay premiums

COMMITMENT CONTRACT – Voluntary agreement to achieve financial savings and rewards for funding HSAs, smoking cessation and improving Bio-Metrics

CONSUMER DRIVEN HEALTH PLAN – Insurance coverage that includes upfront deductibles and other incentives to engage participants to consider the cost of healthcare services, resulting in the elimination of excessive utilization

COINSURANCE – Plan provision where the insured and the plan share a percentage of the cost of services (80% plan & 20% employee)

COORDINATION OF BENEFITS (COB) – Plan provision designed to eliminate duplicate payments for the same service when an employee is covered under two plans

COPAY – Flat dollar payments that are the responsibility of employees to pay a portion of the cost of a service ($20 / $40 / $60)

DEDUCTIBLE – Upfront out-of-pocket expenses that are the employee's responsibility before the insurance plan pays for services ($250 / $500 / $1,000 / $2,000)

ELIGIBLITY PERIOD – The number of days post-employment an individual must wait in order to obtain benefits coverage (90 days for example)

EVIDENCE BASED MEDICINE – A scientific method for assessing the risk and merits of health care treatments, or the lack of treatment

FIDUCIARY – Individual(s) who act in a capacity of trust and exercise discretionary authority over the management of an employee benefit plan

FLEXIBLE SPENDING ACCOUNT (FSA) – Employee per pay deferrals that allow the purchase of qualified health and dependent care services pre-tax

HEALTH CARE EXCHANGE – Government managed online system for purchasing health insurance that includes tax credit

155

subsidies to establish net premium cost based upon income and has plans offered by private insurers labeled Platinum, Gold, Silver, Bronze & High Deductible

HEALTH MAINTENANCE ORGANIZATION (HMO) – A pre-paid medical plan designed to limit access to specific providers for good health and minimized costs

HEALTH REIMBURSEMENT ARRANGEMENT (HRA) – An employer provided benefit designed to offset a portion of deductibles; allows a rollover of unused funds

HEALTH ASSESSMENT – A wellness program questionnaire designed to promote awareness of health risk factors, sometimes referred to as a Health Risk Assessment

HEALTH SAVINGS ACCOUNT (HSA) – Employee owned bank account allowing pre tax deposits to pay qualified health care expenses. Ability to make deposits requires enrollment in a qualified High Deductible Plan

HIPAA – Federal law passed in 1996 establishing privacy and non-discrimination standards

MANAGED CARE – An approach to health cost containment popular in the late 20th and early 21st centuries

OUT-OF-POCKET – The employee personal cost for covered health expenses

OPEN ENROLLMENT – The time period usually up to 60 days prior to a new plan year to make coverage choices

PATIENT PROTECTION & AFFORDABLE CARE ACT (PPACA) – Healthcare reform became law March 23, 2010, and also referred to as "The Affordable Care Act" & "Obamacare". Wealth redistribution, fees, penalties, standardization & government oversight to achieve comprehensive health coverage for all Americans

PAY OR PLAY – Terminology describing an employer's decision to offer health insurance coverage to employees, or pay a penalty to the government

PLAN DOCUMENT – ERISA qualified written description of plan coverage including employee rights

PLAN SPONSOR – The employer that establishes and maintains employee benefit plans

POINT OF SERVICE PLAN (POS) - A pre-paid medical plan like an HMO that includes out of network coverage

PREFERRED PROVIDER ORGANIZATION (PPO) – A network of providers offering discounts on a fee for service basis, freedom of choice & out of network coverage

SELF INSURED – Benefit plans provided by employers who cover enough employees to pay for services as rendered, and maintain their own reserves

STOP LOSS INSURANCE – Employer purchased coverage to limit catastrophic claim exposure for a self- insured medical plan

SSNRA – Social Security Normal Retirement Age access to government benefits at age 67 for persons born in 1960 and later

SUMMARY PLAN DESCRIPTION (SPD) – Benefits booklet providing plan details

THIRD PARTY ADMINISTRATOR (TPA) – Specialized claims processor for self-insured plans

UPFRONT DEDUCTIBLE PLAN – Health insurance coverage with low premiums and a high deductible to be satisfied prior to payments by an insurance company

USUAL, REASONABLE & CUSTOMARY – Prevailing charges from similar providers for health care services

Charts & Commentary

Online Resources

1. IRS on FSA HRA & HSAs www.irs.gov/pub/irs-pdf/p969.pdf

2. US Center for Medicare & Medicaid Services www.cms.hhs.gov/

3. Patient Protection and Affordable Care Act www.dol.gov/ebsa/healthreform

4. International Foundation of Employee Benefit Plans www.ifebp.org/

5. Kaiser Family Foundation   www.kff.org

6. Cardio Kinetics   www.cardiokinetics.com

7. Well Score www.continuancehealthsolutions.com

8. Health Affairs   www.healthaffairs.org

8. DataPath   www.dpath.com

9. JP Warner Associates, Inc. www.warnerbenefits.com

10. Warner Benefits, Inc. www.warnerbenefits.net

11. Human Resource Administrators, Inc. www.hradministrators.com

Jonathan Pierpont Warner, CEBS

No stranger to health care and health insurance, Jon has thirty years of experience consulting employers and individuals on insurance options. He has been a hospital patient six times in his life, most recently in 2012. Jon's wife is a two time cancer survivor and both of his parents lost their lives to cancer while in their early 50's.

Born and raised in the Lehigh Valley, Pennsylvania, he attended Moravian Academy, Liberty High school and is a graduate of Phillips Academy in Andover, Massachusetts, and Middlebury College in Middlebury, Vermont.

Jon is a Certified Employee Benefits Specialist, a graduate education program developed by The International Foundation of Employee Benefit Plans (IFEBP), the International Society of Certified Employee Benefits Specialists (ISCEBS), and the Wharton School of the University of Pennsylvania. He has maintained his Fellowship status with this organization for 12 years.

His entrepreneurial career began following 12 years as a Benefits Consultant and Vice President for regional and national insurance firms. He owns JP Warner Associates, Inc., a brokerage and consulting business and Human Resource Administrators, Inc., a licensed and bonded Third Party Administrator (TPA). Jon is also a partner in Warner Benefits, Inc. with his brother Andrew. These businesses offer employee benefits consulting, insurance brokerage, claims administration, retirement planning and investment services to more than 300 employers.

Jon's first published work in 1989 was an educational piece on HMO legislation. He next authored a white paper called "FROM MANAGED CARE TO FINANCED CARE" published in 2002. His first book <u>MAKING $ENSE OF 21st CENTURY HEALTH PLANS</u> was published in 2009.

Inspiration for his new book <u>HOW TO WIN THE HEALTH CARE GAME</u> culminated as a growing list of clients and individuals have tempered health care cost increases by adopting strategies that include upfront deductible plans with HRAs, FSAs and, or HSAs. Reining in health insurance expenses using this creative approach allows for the continuation of quality insurance benefits while increasing take home pay for workers. Jon is a frequent public speaker who remains hopeful the number of American workers with Health Savings Accounts will continue to increase. Jon has $30,000 saved so far in his HSA, with plans to grow it beyond $100,000.

Married for 25 years, Jon and his wife are raising three wonderful children. They live in suburban Philadelphia, PA. Jon sings at his church, interviews applicants interested in attending Middlebury College, and is the Vice Chairman for the J. Wood Platt Caddie Scholarship Trust, which helps defray college tuition costs for golf caddies. He is also a member of the C12 Group of Christian business owners and CEOs, which inspired him to complete his goal to author a book explaining health insurance history, legislative trends and forward thinking concepts about high quality, efficient insurance protection.